Energy Security and Sustainable Development: Advancing Clean Energy, Climate Change Action, Renewable Energy, Energy Efficiency, Global Policy, and Green Finance

I0022949

Copyright

Energy Security and Sustainable Development: Advancing Clean Energy, Climate Change Action, Renewable Energy, Energy Efficiency, Global Policy, and Green Finance

© 2025 Robert C. Brears

ISBN (eBook): 978-1-991368-47-8

ISBN (Paperback): 978-1-991368-48-5

Published by Global Climate Solutions

First Edition, 2025

Cover design and interior layout by Global Climate Solutions

Table of Contents

Introduction

Energy security lies at the core of sustainable development. It represents the ability of societies to access reliable, affordable, and sustainable energy to meet present and future needs. Without secure energy supplies, progress in reducing poverty, advancing healthcare, improving education, and achieving industrial growth becomes constrained. At the same time, energy production and use are major drivers of environmental change, making energy security a cross-cutting issue that influences economic, social, and ecological systems.

Global energy demand continues to rise due to population growth, industrialization, and urbanization. This growth increases pressure on natural resources and infrastructure while intensifying greenhouse gas emissions. The challenge is not only to ensure sufficient energy supply but also to transition to cleaner systems that align with the Sustainable Development Goals (SDGs). The SDGs emphasize universal access to modern energy (SDG 7), but achieving this target also supports many others, including climate action, clean water, sustainable cities, and responsible consumption.

Energy security has evolved beyond concerns of supply disruptions or price volatility. It now encompasses resilience to environmental, technological, and geopolitical risks. Extreme weather events threaten energy infrastructure, cyberattacks endanger digitalized grids, and shifting global alliances reshape energy trade patterns. Ensuring stability in this context requires diversification of sources, enhanced system flexibility, and strategic investment in innovation and efficiency.

Sustainable energy transitions offer opportunities to strengthen energy security while contributing to global development goals. Renewable energy technologies, energy efficiency measures, and smart systems can reduce dependency on fossil fuels and improve access in remote regions. Integrating these approaches requires coherent policies, strong institutions, and financial mechanisms that encourage both innovation and inclusion.

International cooperation is fundamental. Energy challenges transcend borders, and global initiatives play a key role in fostering technological transfer, capacity building, and financial support for developing nations. A secure and sustainable energy future depends on equitable participation, where countries collaborate to share knowledge and resources rather than compete for them.

This book examines how energy security connects with the SDGs through policy, technology, and governance. It explores pathways that balance economic growth with environmental limits and social progress. Each chapter addresses a dimension of this intersection, from universal access and efficiency to finance, governance, and resilience. Together, they provide insights into how energy systems can evolve to meet global development needs while ensuring long-term stability and sustainability.

Chapter 1: The Nexus Between Energy Security and Sustainable Development

Energy security and sustainable development are interconnected goals that shape global economic, social, and environmental outcomes. Energy security ensures that societies have access to reliable and affordable energy to power industries, transport, and households, while sustainable development emphasizes the responsible use of resources to meet current needs without compromising future generations. The nexus between these two concepts highlights the need for integrated strategies that balance growth, equity, and environmental protection. Understanding this relationship is essential for designing energy systems that advance human well-being, promote resilience, and contribute to achieving the Sustainable Development Goals.

Defining Energy Security in a Global Context

Energy security refers to the uninterrupted availability of energy sources at an affordable price while maintaining environmental and social sustainability. It involves ensuring that societies can meet their energy needs reliably, affordably, and equitably. In today's interconnected world, energy security extends beyond national boundaries and encompasses global supply chains, technological innovation, and international cooperation. The concept has evolved over time, reflecting changes in the global economy, environmental priorities, and technological capabilities.

Historically, energy security was primarily concerned with ensuring a stable supply of fossil fuels, particularly oil. The oil crises of the 1970s demonstrated the vulnerability of economies dependent on imported energy and shaped decades of national energy policy. Over time, the scope of energy security expanded to include electricity, natural gas, renewables, and critical raw materials essential for energy systems. It now integrates environmental concerns and social dimensions, recognizing that reliable energy access is vital to sustainable development.

Energy security is multidimensional. Its key dimensions include availability, accessibility, affordability, and acceptability. Availability refers to the physical existence of energy resources and the infrastructure to produce, transport, and deliver them. Accessibility concerns the ability of countries and consumers to obtain energy, influenced by market conditions, geopolitical stability, and policy frameworks. Affordability relates to the cost of energy and its impact on economic competitiveness and social equity. Acceptability addresses environmental and social implications, emphasizing sustainability, safety, and public trust.

The global nature of energy markets adds complexity to the concept of security. Energy production and consumption are unevenly distributed across the world, leading to dependence between producers and consumers. Countries that import large shares of their energy are exposed to geopolitical risks and price volatility. Exporting nations face their own vulnerabilities, such as fluctuating demand or shifts in technology that reduce reliance on their resources. The interconnectedness of supply chains means that disruptions in one region can have worldwide effects.

Technological innovation has redefined what constitutes energy security. The rise of renewable energy, storage technologies, and digital systems has diversified supply sources and reduced exposure to traditional risks. However, these innovations also introduce new dependencies on minerals such as lithium, cobalt, and rare earth elements, creating fresh vulnerabilities. The integration of digital technologies enhances system efficiency and resilience but also introduces risks from cyber threats and data breaches. Managing these trade-offs requires forward-looking strategies that consider both traditional and emerging risks.

Climate change has become a defining factor in energy security. Extreme weather events, droughts, and rising sea levels can disrupt energy supply chains, damage infrastructure, and affect resource availability. Ensuring energy security now involves building resilience to these environmental stresses. Transitioning to low-carbon energy systems also creates challenges for countries reliant on fossil fuel exports, demanding policies that manage social and economic adjustments while maintaining stability.

Energy security is closely linked to social equity and inclusion. Access to affordable and reliable energy underpins livelihoods, education, healthcare, and overall human well-being. Millions of people still lack access to modern energy services, particularly in developing regions. Addressing this inequity is fundamental to achieving sustainable energy security. Policies must balance the goals of expanding access, reducing emissions, and ensuring affordability for vulnerable populations.

Governments and international organizations have developed various frameworks to assess and promote energy security. Indicators often measure diversification of supply, efficiency of infrastructure, energy intensity, and the share of renewables in the mix. Global initiatives such as the International Energy Agency (IEA) and the United Nations Sustainable Energy for All (SEforALL) initiative promote cooperation and knowledge sharing. These efforts aim to build resilience through diversification, innovation, and efficiency improvements across all sectors of the energy system.

Energy security must also account for long-term transitions. The shift toward renewable and decentralized systems changes how energy is produced, distributed, and consumed. Local generation, smart grids, and storage technologies enhance reliability and reduce exposure to global market fluctuations. However, this transformation requires substantial investment, institutional reform, and social acceptance. Policymakers must create stable and transparent frameworks that encourage investment while protecting consumers and the environment.

In a globalized and rapidly changing world, energy security encompasses both the prevention of short-term disruptions and the capacity to adapt to long-term structural changes. It requires coordination among governments, industries, and communities to balance economic competitiveness, environmental sustainability, and social inclusion. Energy security, once viewed primarily through the lens of national sovereignty, has become a shared global responsibility shaped by cooperation, innovation, and resilience.

The Role of Energy in Achieving the SDGs

Energy plays an essential role in advancing global development by enabling progress across all sectors of society. The Sustainable Development Goals (SDGs) recognize this interconnection through SDG 7, which aims to ensure access to affordable, reliable, sustainable, and modern energy for all. Achieving SDG 7 underpins the realization of nearly every other SDG, as energy influences economic growth, social inclusion, environmental protection, and institutional capacity. Reliable energy access allows economies to function efficiently, supports innovation, and enhances the quality of life, making it a central enabler of sustainable development.

Economic growth is directly linked to energy availability and use. Industries depend on stable energy supplies to operate machinery, process raw materials, and transport goods. Energy drives productivity in agriculture, manufacturing, and services, supporting employment and income generation. In developing countries, expanding access to electricity facilitates the creation of new enterprises and stimulates investment in infrastructure. Modern energy also enhances competitiveness by improving operational efficiency and reducing production costs. The challenge lies in balancing economic expansion with the need to minimize environmental impacts and manage resource constraints.

Energy access improves living standards by providing essential services that promote health, education, and social well-being. Electricity enables hospitals to deliver reliable medical care, schools to offer digital learning, and households to benefit from clean cooking and heating. Replacing traditional biomass fuels with cleaner alternatives reduces indoor air pollution and associated health risks. Reliable energy also supports the operation of water supply systems, sanitation networks, and emergency response services. As societies urbanize, energy demand grows rapidly, and ensuring equitable access becomes essential to reducing inequality and promoting social inclusion.

The transition to sustainable energy systems contributes to environmental protection and climate stability. Renewable energy sources such as solar, wind, and hydropower reduce dependence on fossil fuels and lower greenhouse gas emissions. Improving energy efficiency across industrial, transport, and residential sectors helps decouple economic growth from environmental degradation. These actions directly support SDG 13 on climate action, while also contributing to goals related to clean water, sustainable cities, and responsible consumption. Integrating renewable energy into national energy systems requires policy coordination, technological innovation, and infrastructure investment.

Energy security is critical to achieving the SDGs because it ensures the stability of essential services and economic activities. Disruptions in supply, price volatility, or infrastructure failures can have far-reaching consequences for development outcomes. Strengthening energy security involves diversifying energy sources, investing in resilient infrastructure, and improving efficiency in energy use. For developing economies, building local generation capacity and enhancing regional interconnections can reduce dependency on imports and improve supply reliability. Long-term energy planning that integrates climate and social considerations is essential for maintaining stability and advancing sustainable development.

Gender equality and social inclusion benefit directly from improved energy access. In many regions, women and girls spend significant time collecting traditional fuels, limiting their opportunities for education and employment. Access to modern energy reduces this burden and supports gender equality by enabling participation in economic activities and community decision-making. Electrification of schools and health centers improves outcomes for women and children, contributing to broader social progress. Energy policies that prioritize inclusiveness and affordability help ensure that marginalized communities benefit equally from development gains.

Innovation in energy systems accelerates progress toward multiple SDGs. Advances in renewable technologies, energy storage, and smart grids enhance efficiency and expand access in remote or underserved areas. Digital solutions such as smart metering, demand response systems, and data analytics improve management of energy resources. These innovations also create opportunities for green jobs, supporting SDG 8 on decent work and economic growth. Research and development play a crucial role in driving down costs and scaling up clean technologies that make sustainable energy transitions viable across diverse contexts.

Finance and investment are vital components of achieving energy-related SDGs. Expanding access to modern energy and deploying renewable technologies require significant capital, particularly in developing regions. Mobilizing finance through public–private partnerships, green bonds, and international climate funds can accelerate progress. Policies that create stable markets, reduce investment risks, and promote transparency attract long-term investment in sustainable energy projects. International cooperation and capacity building help bridge financing gaps and ensure that developing countries can adopt modern energy systems aligned with global sustainability goals.

Energy connects directly and indirectly with all 17 SDGs. It supports poverty reduction by enabling economic opportunities, enhances food security through mechanization and cold storage, and improves water management through pumping and desalination. In cities, sustainable energy solutions contribute to cleaner transport and reduced emissions. In rural areas, decentralized energy systems strengthen community resilience and productivity. By integrating energy considerations across all development strategies, countries can create synergies that accelerate progress toward a sustainable and equitable global future.

Interdependencies Between Energy, Water, Food, and Climate

Energy, water, food, and climate systems are deeply interconnected, forming a complex nexus that underpins global sustainability. Each element depends on and influences the others, meaning that decisions in one sector can have significant consequences across the rest. Understanding these interdependencies is crucial for designing policies that balance economic growth, environmental protection, and social well-being. The integration of these systems is essential to achieving long-term resource security and advancing sustainable development.

Energy production requires substantial quantities of water for extraction, processing, and cooling. Thermal power plants rely on water for cooling, while hydropower depends entirely on water availability. Bioenergy crops compete with agriculture for irrigation and land, and oil and gas extraction often involve water-intensive processes. As water resources become increasingly stressed by population growth, pollution, and climate change, the security of energy systems is directly affected. Efficient water management within the energy sector reduces vulnerability and supports system reliability.

Water supply and treatment, in turn, depend heavily on energy. Pumping, desalination, and wastewater treatment require electricity and fuel to operate. In many regions, water utilities are among the largest consumers of energy, making them sensitive to fluctuations in energy prices and availability. Improving energy efficiency in water systems reduces operational costs and emissions, while renewable-powered water infrastructure enhances sustainability. Integrating energy and water planning ensures that resource use is optimized across both sectors.

The food system also has strong linkages with energy and water. Agriculture consumes the majority of global freshwater resources, with irrigation systems often powered by fossil fuels or electricity.

Energy is required throughout the food supply chain, from fertilizer production and mechanized farming to processing, transport, and refrigeration. Rising energy costs or shortages can therefore affect food production, distribution, and prices. At the same time, inefficient water and energy use in agriculture contributes to environmental degradation, including soil depletion and water scarcity.

Climate change intensifies the challenges within the energy-water-food nexus. Shifting temperature and precipitation patterns affect water availability, crop yields, and energy production. Droughts reduce hydropower generation and cooling capacity for thermal plants, while floods can damage energy and agricultural infrastructure. Climate-related disruptions to one resource system can cascade through others, amplifying risks to economies and communities. Addressing these interconnected vulnerabilities requires integrated adaptation and mitigation strategies.

Renewable energy can help reduce pressure on water and food systems, though its deployment must be managed carefully. Solar and wind energy typically have lower water footprints than fossil fuel-based systems, but the production of their components and materials can still involve significant resource use. Bioenergy presents both opportunities and risks, depending on how land and water are managed. Strategic planning that considers full lifecycle impacts helps prevent unintended consequences and promotes resource efficiency across the nexus.

Technological innovation plays a vital role in enhancing the sustainability of interlinked systems. Advances such as precision irrigation, wastewater reuse, and renewable-powered desalination improve efficiency and resilience. Integrating data from remote sensing, artificial intelligence, and digital platforms enables real-time monitoring of water, energy, and agricultural systems. These tools support informed decision-making and facilitate the coordination of resource management across sectors and scales.

Governance frameworks are central to managing nexus interdependencies. Institutional fragmentation often leads to conflicting policies and inefficient resource allocation. Coordinated governance that aligns water, energy, and agricultural policies reduces trade-offs and promotes synergies. Cross-sectoral planning, stakeholder engagement, and transparent data sharing strengthen policy coherence. International cooperation further supports the exchange of knowledge and technologies that enhance integrated management.

Financial and policy mechanisms can accelerate the transition to a more efficient and resilient nexus. Investments in sustainable infrastructure, circular economy solutions, and nature-based approaches reduce resource demand and enhance system flexibility. Pricing reforms that reflect the true value of resources encourage efficiency while supporting equitable access. Aligning financial incentives with sustainability goals ensures that development pathways remain consistent with climate and environmental commitments.

The interdependencies between energy, water, food, and climate highlight the need for holistic approaches that transcend traditional policy boundaries. Integrating these systems through coherent strategies enhances resource efficiency, reduces risks, and supports progress toward sustainable development.

Policy Coherence and Integrated Frameworks

Policy coherence and integrated frameworks are essential for aligning energy security objectives with broader sustainable development goals. Fragmented policymaking can lead to conflicting priorities, inefficiencies, and unintended consequences across sectors such as water, agriculture, transport, and industry. Coordinated policies ensure that energy-related decisions contribute to economic growth, environmental protection, and social inclusion in a balanced and efficient manner.

Effective policy coherence begins with establishing clear national visions and strategies that integrate energy security within the context of the Sustainable Development Goals (SDGs). These strategies require collaboration across ministries, regulatory bodies, and local authorities to ensure consistency between economic, environmental, and social policies. Institutional coordination mechanisms, such as inter-ministerial committees or national councils for sustainable development, facilitate communication and prevent duplication of efforts. By embedding sustainability objectives into long-term energy planning, governments can align short-term actions with long-term development outcomes.

Integrated policy frameworks rely on cross-sectoral planning that addresses the interdependencies between energy and other resources. For instance, energy policies must account for water use in energy production, while agricultural and industrial policies should consider energy demand. Land-use planning also plays a role, as renewable energy expansion competes with agriculture and biodiversity conservation. Developing shared data systems and analytical tools helps identify synergies and trade-offs, allowing policymakers to design strategies that optimize resource use and reduce conflicts among sectors.

International cooperation strengthens policy coherence by promoting shared standards, knowledge exchange, and financial support. Multilateral frameworks such as the Paris Agreement and regional energy initiatives encourage countries to harmonize policies and adopt consistent regulatory approaches. Cooperation on transboundary infrastructure, such as power grids and pipelines, enhances energy security and market integration. Global partnerships also help mobilize resources and technical expertise, particularly for developing nations seeking to advance both energy access and sustainability.

Regulatory frameworks play a central role in translating policy coherence into actionable outcomes. Clear and predictable regulations create stable environments for investment, while flexible mechanisms allow adaptation to technological and market changes.

Energy pricing policies, including subsidies and taxes, should reflect environmental and social costs to promote efficiency and equity. Transparent governance structures enhance accountability, ensuring that policies are implemented effectively and in the public interest.

Integrated frameworks also depend on inclusive stakeholder engagement. Engaging the private sector, civil society, and local communities ensures that policies address diverse needs and perspectives. Participatory approaches increase legitimacy, build trust, and enhance compliance. Localized policy design allows for context-specific solutions, especially in decentralized energy systems where community ownership and participation play a growing role.

Monitoring and evaluation mechanisms are necessary for maintaining policy coherence over time. Tracking progress through performance indicators and feedback loops enables continuous improvement. Evaluating policies based on economic, environmental, and social outcomes helps identify gaps and refine strategies. Integrating adaptive management approaches ensures that frameworks remain responsive to emerging challenges such as climate change, technological innovation, and shifting market dynamics.

Policy coherence and integrated frameworks provide the structure needed to manage the complexity of modern energy systems. Aligning objectives across sectors and governance levels reduces inefficiencies, mitigates risks, and promotes sustainable development outcomes consistent with global energy and climate goals.

Chapter 2: Universal Energy Access and the SDG 7 Agenda

Universal access to affordable, reliable, sustainable, and modern energy is a cornerstone of the Sustainable Development Goals, captured in SDG 7. Energy access underpins progress across multiple dimensions of development, from health and education to gender equality and economic growth. Yet, significant disparities persist between and within countries, particularly in rural and low-income regions where millions remain without electricity or clean cooking solutions. Expanding access requires a combination of policy innovation, investment, and technology deployment. This chapter examines the global effort to achieve SDG 7, exploring pathways to deliver inclusive and sustainable energy systems for all.

Energy Poverty and Development Outcomes

Energy poverty refers to the lack of access to modern energy services that are essential for economic and social development. It includes limited or no access to electricity, reliance on traditional biomass for cooking and heating, and the inability to afford sufficient energy for basic needs. Energy poverty affects billions of people globally, primarily in developing regions, where inadequate infrastructure and low income levels restrict access to reliable and affordable energy. Addressing energy poverty is fundamental to achieving sustainable development and improving quality of life.

Electricity access is a key driver of economic progress. It enables industries to operate efficiently, supports small businesses, and promotes job creation. In rural areas, electrification stimulates local economies by facilitating the development of agro-processing, cold storage, and other value-added activities. Households with access to electricity can extend working and study hours, improving productivity and educational outcomes. However, in many regions, energy access remains uneven, with rural and low-income populations facing persistent barriers due to high costs, geographic isolation, or inadequate grid infrastructure.

Lack of access to modern energy has profound implications for health and well-being. Dependence on solid fuels such as wood, charcoal, and dung for cooking and heating exposes households to indoor air pollution, leading to respiratory illnesses and premature deaths. Women and children are disproportionately affected, as they spend more time near cooking stoves. Modern energy access enables the use of cleaner cooking technologies, improved ventilation, and reliable electricity for healthcare facilities. Electrified clinics can provide essential services such as refrigeration for vaccines, sterilization of equipment, and operation of medical devices, contributing to better public health outcomes.

Energy poverty also limits educational opportunities. In areas without reliable electricity, schools cannot provide lighting, digital learning tools, or modern teaching equipment. Students struggle to study after dark, and teachers face constraints in delivering quality education. Electrification enhances learning environments and facilitates access to information and communication technologies that connect students to global knowledge networks. By improving education, energy access supports long-term economic and social development and empowers communities to participate more fully in national economies.

Gender inequality is closely linked to energy poverty. In many developing countries, women and girls are responsible for collecting firewood and other fuels, often spending several hours each day on this task. This reduces time available for education, income-generating activities, and community participation. Access to modern energy alleviates this burden by enabling cleaner cooking technologies, mechanized water pumping, and improved household appliances. When women have access to energy, they gain opportunities to start businesses, access information, and engage in leadership roles, contributing to gender equality and social progress.

Energy affordability is another critical dimension of energy poverty. Even when physical infrastructure exists, high tariffs and connection costs can prevent low-income households from gaining access. In many urban areas, informal settlements lack legal connections, forcing residents to rely on unsafe or expensive alternatives. Policies that promote targeted subsidies, microfinance, or pay-as-you-go systems can help make energy services more affordable. Expanding decentralized renewable energy solutions, such as solar home systems and mini-grids, offers viable alternatives where traditional grid expansion is not cost-effective.

Energy poverty has significant implications for agricultural productivity and food security. Farmers rely on energy for irrigation, mechanization, storage, and transportation of produce. Without reliable energy, agricultural activities remain labor-intensive and vulnerable to losses from spoilage. Access to modern energy allows for more efficient water use, improved crop yields, and value addition through processing and preservation. This, in turn, supports rural livelihoods and reduces poverty in communities that depend heavily on agriculture.

The persistence of energy poverty also affects national competitiveness and social stability. Countries with limited access to energy face constraints in industrialization, innovation, and economic diversification. Energy shortages disrupt production, discourage investment, and limit the capacity of governments to deliver public services. Expanding access to reliable and sustainable energy strengthens national resilience and creates conditions for inclusive growth. Integrating energy access into national development planning ensures that progress is equitable and aligned with broader sustainability objectives.

Addressing energy poverty requires coordinated action across multiple sectors. Governments, international organizations, and private actors must work together to expand infrastructure, mobilize finance, and develop policies that promote equitable access. Investment in renewable energy technologies plays a critical role, offering decentralized and low-cost solutions for underserved populations. Strengthening institutions, regulatory frameworks, and data systems helps ensure that energy access initiatives are effective and sustainable.

Eliminating energy poverty is not solely a technical challenge but also a social and economic priority. Ensuring universal access to modern energy enables progress across education, health, gender equality, and environmental protection. Reducing energy poverty strengthens human development, enhances resilience, and supports the transition toward sustainable and inclusive growth.

Electrification Pathways: Grid, Mini-Grid, and Off-Grid Solutions

Expanding electricity access is central to addressing energy poverty and achieving sustainable development. Different electrification pathways—grid, mini-grid, and off-grid systems—offer complementary approaches to extending reliable and affordable electricity to diverse populations. Each pathway has unique advantages and challenges depending on geographic conditions, population density, infrastructure capacity, and institutional frameworks. Selecting the appropriate mix of solutions requires integrated planning and adaptive policy frameworks that reflect local needs and long-term sustainability goals.

Grid-based electrification remains the primary method for delivering large-scale and reliable electricity supply. National grids provide economies of scale, enabling centralized generation, transmission, and distribution of electricity across regions. Expanding the main grid can connect urban centers and industrial zones, supporting economic growth and modernization. However, in many developing countries, extending the grid to remote or sparsely populated areas can be economically and technically challenging. High infrastructure costs, difficult terrain, and low electricity demand in rural areas often limit the financial viability of grid expansion. Strengthening the existing grid through modernization, smart technologies, and renewable integration can improve reliability and efficiency.

Mini-grids represent a flexible and scalable solution for communities that are not yet connected to the national grid. These localized systems generate and distribute electricity independently, using a combination of renewable sources such as solar, wind, hydro, or biomass, and sometimes diesel backup for reliability. Mini-grids can serve small towns, industrial clusters, or agricultural communities, providing consistent power for households and local businesses. Advances in digital metering, battery storage, and remote monitoring have enhanced their operational performance and cost-effectiveness. Regulatory support and clear frameworks for interconnection with national grids encourage investment and enable future integration when grid extension becomes feasible.

Off-grid systems provide immediate and low-cost solutions for dispersed or isolated populations. Solar home systems, standalone micro-hydro plants, and portable renewable devices deliver essential services such as lighting, phone charging, and small appliance operation. These systems are particularly valuable in regions where conventional grid or mini-grid expansion is not economically viable. Declining costs of solar panels and batteries have made off-grid technologies increasingly accessible, supported by innovative financing models such as pay-as-you-go schemes. While off-grid systems may not initially provide the same power capacity as grid-based solutions, they play a vital role in achieving universal energy access and improving living standards in underserved communities.

Hybrid approaches that combine grid, mini-grid, and off-grid systems can create a more resilient and adaptive electrification framework. Integrated planning allows governments and utilities to deploy each solution where it is most effective while maintaining consistency with national energy strategies. For example, off-grid and mini-grid systems can serve as transitional or complementary solutions before grid connection, ensuring no community is left behind. Coordinating investment, regulation, and technology standards across all three systems promotes interoperability and long-term sustainability.

Policy and regulatory environments are key determinants of successful electrification pathways. Clear frameworks that define technical standards, pricing structures, and interconnection rules attract private investment and reduce uncertainty. Incentives for renewable energy deployment, streamlined licensing processes, and financial mechanisms such as subsidies or guarantees can accelerate project implementation. Institutional coordination between energy authorities, utilities, and local governments ensures that electrification strategies align with national development and climate objectives.

Financing remains a critical challenge for large-scale electrification. Public funding alone is insufficient to meet investment needs, making private sector participation essential. Blended finance models that combine public, private, and donor resources can help mitigate risks and mobilize capital for infrastructure development. Decentralized energy systems, particularly mini-grids and off-grid solutions, offer opportunities for small-scale entrepreneurs and local communities to participate in energy markets, fostering inclusiveness and local ownership.

Technological innovation continues to shape the future of electrification. Smart grids, energy storage, and digital platforms enhance system efficiency, flexibility, and customer engagement. Data-driven planning tools enable policymakers to identify the most cost-effective pathways and optimize resource allocation. Integrating renewable energy into all electrification modes supports environmental goals while improving energy security.

Electrification pathways that combine grid, mini-grid, and off-grid systems offer a comprehensive approach to achieving universal access. Strategic coordination, supportive policies, and investment in innovation are essential to delivering reliable, affordable, and sustainable electricity for all.

Clean Cooking and Household Energy Transition

Clean cooking and household energy transitions are vital for improving public health, reducing environmental degradation, and achieving sustainable development. In many parts of the world, especially in low- and middle-income countries, households still rely on traditional biomass such as wood, charcoal, dung, and crop residues for cooking and heating. These fuels are often burned in inefficient stoves or open fires, producing harmful smoke and particulate matter that pose severe health and environmental risks. Transitioning to clean cooking solutions is essential for advancing energy access, gender equality, and climate objectives.

Traditional cooking practices contribute significantly to household air pollution, which is one of the leading causes of premature deaths globally. Exposure to smoke from solid fuels increases the risk of respiratory diseases, heart conditions, and eye problems. Women and children are the most affected, as they spend more time near cooking areas. Clean cooking technologies—such as improved biomass stoves, liquefied petroleum gas (LPG), biogas, ethanol, and electric cookers—can drastically reduce indoor air pollution and improve health outcomes. Public health benefits from such transitions extend beyond individual households to community well-being and healthcare systems.

Environmental impacts of traditional cooking are substantial. Unsustainable harvesting of firewood and charcoal production contributes to deforestation, soil erosion, and biodiversity loss. The carbon emissions resulting from inefficient fuel combustion also exacerbate climate change. Clean cooking solutions offer opportunities to reduce emissions and pressure on ecosystems. For example, biogas systems utilize organic waste to produce renewable energy, while electric cooking powered by renewable grids or solar systems eliminates local pollution and contributes to decarbonization. Integrating clean cooking initiatives into climate and energy policies enhances environmental sustainability while supporting national commitments to emission reduction.

The economic implications of household energy transitions are far-reaching. Traditional fuels require considerable time and effort to collect, limiting productivity and economic participation, particularly among women. The shift to modern fuels and technologies reduces this burden and enables households to redirect time toward education, employment, and entrepreneurship. Access to affordable and efficient cooking solutions also reduces household expenditure over time by lowering fuel consumption. Expanding clean cooking markets can stimulate job creation in manufacturing, distribution, and maintenance of modern stoves and fuels, fostering inclusive economic growth.

Energy affordability remains a critical barrier to widespread adoption of clean cooking technologies. High upfront costs for equipment, unreliable fuel supply chains, and limited financing options restrict access for low-income households. Policy interventions such as targeted subsidies, microcredit programs, and public–private partnerships can bridge affordability gaps. Innovative business models, including pay-as-you-go and community-based distribution networks, have proven effective in scaling up access to modern cooking technologies. Ensuring affordability and availability of clean fuels requires coordinated efforts between governments, financial institutions, and the private sector.

Social and cultural factors also influence the pace of the household energy transition. Cooking practices are deeply rooted in local traditions, tastes, and lifestyles. Successful programs for clean cooking adoption must consider these preferences through user-centered design and community engagement. Education and awareness campaigns are essential to demonstrate the health, economic, and environmental benefits of modern cooking methods. Empowering women as advocates and entrepreneurs in clean cooking initiatives strengthens both social acceptance and gender equality.

Technological innovation continues to expand the range of clean cooking options. Electric pressure cookers, induction stoves, and advanced biomass gasifiers offer efficient and user-friendly alternatives to traditional systems. Integration of digital technologies allows for improved monitoring of usage patterns, enabling better targeting of subsidies and support programs. Investment in research and development accelerates cost reductions and enhances performance, ensuring that technologies remain affordable and adaptable to local conditions.

The household energy transition is a cornerstone of achieving universal energy access and advancing multiple Sustainable Development Goals. Expanding clean cooking solutions improves health, protects the environment, supports gender equality, and enhances economic opportunity. Coordinated policies, financing mechanisms, and inclusive implementation strategies are essential for enabling every household to access safe, reliable, and sustainable cooking energy.

Financing Universal Access and the Role of Public–Private Partnerships

Financing universal energy access is one of the most significant challenges in achieving sustainable development. Expanding electricity and clean cooking access to underserved populations requires large-scale investment in infrastructure, technology, and capacity building. Public resources alone are insufficient to meet the financing gap, making the mobilization of private capital and innovative funding mechanisms essential. Public–private partnerships (PPPs) provide a structured approach to leverage the strengths of both sectors, combining public oversight with private sector efficiency, innovation, and investment capacity.

Universal energy access demands long-term financial planning and stable policy environments. Governments play a central role in creating enabling conditions for investment through sound regulatory frameworks, transparent procurement processes, and credible policy commitments. Clear national electrification strategies that integrate grid, mini-grid, and off-grid solutions guide investment priorities and help attract both domestic and international investors. Establishing independent regulatory bodies and ensuring predictable tariff regimes increase investor confidence by reducing political and financial risks.

The financing requirements for universal access are substantial and vary by region and technology. Extending the main electricity grid involves high capital costs, particularly in remote areas with low population density. Mini-grid and off-grid systems require smaller investments but often face challenges related to scale, affordability, and long-term maintenance. Blended finance, which combines public, private, and concessional funding, can help close these gaps by reducing perceived risks and improving project bankability. Development finance institutions and multilateral organizations play a key role in structuring such arrangements and providing guarantees, loans, and technical assistance.

Public investment remains essential for expanding energy access in areas where market conditions are weak or returns are uncertain. Governments can allocate funds for infrastructure development, provide targeted subsidies for low-income households, and support research and development of new technologies. Public funding is also critical for building institutional capacity and establishing monitoring systems to ensure accountability and transparency. Strategic public spending can crowd in private investment by improving the overall investment climate and demonstrating government commitment to sustainable energy goals.

Private sector participation introduces efficiency, innovation, and operational expertise into energy access initiatives. Companies can design, finance, build, and operate energy systems while governments provide regulatory oversight and performance monitoring. PPPs allow for risk sharing, where public entities mitigate certain risks such as demand fluctuations or currency volatility, while private partners assume responsibility for project implementation and maintenance. This model has proven effective in scaling up renewable energy projects, developing decentralized systems, and modernizing infrastructure.

Innovative financing instruments are expanding opportunities for private investment in energy access. Green bonds, sustainability-linked loans, and impact investment funds channel capital toward environmentally and socially beneficial projects. Results-based financing, where payments are linked to verified outcomes, incentivizes performance and accountability. Pay-as-you-go models supported by mobile payment systems enable households to access energy services without high upfront costs, improving affordability and expanding market reach. Digital platforms that track energy usage and financial flows enhance transparency and investor confidence.

Community participation and local entrepreneurship are important components of financing strategies. Decentralized energy systems, such as solar mini-grids and home systems, create opportunities for local ownership and management. Supporting small and medium-sized enterprises through microfinance, grants, or concessional loans helps generate employment and fosters inclusive economic growth. Capacity building and technical training strengthen local institutions and ensure the long-term sustainability of investments.

International cooperation and climate finance play critical roles in achieving universal energy access. Global initiatives such as Sustainable Energy for All (SEforALL) and the Green Climate Fund (GCF) mobilize resources and facilitate technology transfer to developing countries. Donor governments, multilateral banks, and private investors can align efforts to support national energy access plans and promote equitable distribution of benefits. Transparent coordination among international stakeholders enhances efficiency and ensures that resources are directed where they are most needed.

A combination of public funding, private investment, and international cooperation forms the foundation for achieving universal energy access. Public–private partnerships, supported by sound policies and innovative financing mechanisms, provide the structure necessary to mobilize capital, manage risk, and deliver sustainable energy solutions to all communities.

Chapter 3: Energy Efficiency for Economic Growth and Environmental Sustainability

Energy efficiency plays a critical role in promoting sustainable economic growth and reducing environmental impact. By optimizing energy use across industries, buildings, and transport systems, countries can lower costs, improve competitiveness, and minimize greenhouse gas emissions. Efficiency improvements reduce pressure on natural resources while enhancing energy security through lower demand and reduced import dependence. As economies expand, the need to decouple growth from energy consumption becomes increasingly urgent. This chapter explores how energy efficiency serves as a driver of productivity, innovation, and climate mitigation, outlining strategies that balance economic development with environmental stewardship.

The Efficiency Imperative in Global Energy Systems

Energy efficiency is a cornerstone of sustainable development, enabling countries to reduce energy demand while maintaining economic growth and improving quality of life. It serves as the first and most cost-effective step toward achieving energy security, climate goals, and resource conservation. Enhancing efficiency across all sectors—industry, transport, buildings, and power generation—reduces reliance on fossil fuels, lowers emissions, and minimizes the need for new infrastructure investment.

Improving energy efficiency enhances energy security by reducing the amount of energy required to support economic and social activities. Countries that rely heavily on energy imports can lower their exposure to volatile global prices and supply disruptions through efficiency improvements. Energy savings in end-use sectors, such as transportation and manufacturing, free up capacity for other uses and delay the need for new generation assets. Efficiency measures, when combined with renewable energy, help create a stable and diversified energy system that supports long-term economic resilience.

In industrial sectors, efficiency improvements reduce operational costs and increase competitiveness. Many industries depend on energy-intensive processes, such as steelmaking, cement production, and chemicals manufacturing. Adopting high-efficiency motors, waste heat recovery, and advanced process optimization technologies can significantly lower energy intensity. Digitalization and automation further enhance monitoring and control of industrial systems, enabling real-time adjustments that maximize efficiency. These measures contribute not only to lower energy costs but also to reduced carbon footprints across supply chains.

The building sector represents one of the largest opportunities for efficiency gains. Residential and commercial buildings account for a substantial share of global energy consumption, primarily through heating, cooling, lighting, and appliances. Implementing energy-efficient building designs, insulation, and smart technologies can drastically reduce consumption. Policies such as mandatory energy performance standards, labeling schemes, and incentives for retrofitting existing structures encourage widespread adoption. Urban planning that prioritizes compact, well-connected communities reduces overall energy demand in transportation and public services.

Transport systems are another key area for energy efficiency improvement. The sector's dependence on fossil fuels makes it a major source of greenhouse gas emissions. Transitioning to electric mobility, improving vehicle fuel efficiency, and promoting public transport and non-motorized mobility reduce both energy consumption and emissions. Advanced logistics management and digital technologies optimize routes and freight operations, cutting unnecessary energy use. Integration of renewable energy in transport infrastructure, such as electric vehicle charging networks powered by solar or wind energy, supports cleaner and more efficient mobility systems.

The power generation and transmission sectors play a crucial role in enhancing system-wide efficiency. Upgrading power plants, reducing transmission and distribution losses, and integrating smart grid technologies improve the overall performance of energy systems. The shift toward combined heat and power (CHP) systems increases efficiency by utilizing waste heat from electricity generation. Demand-side management programs enable utilities to balance load, reducing the need for expensive peak generation capacity. Investments in digital infrastructure and data analytics allow better forecasting and grid optimization, supporting reliable and efficient energy delivery.

Energy efficiency is also a powerful tool for reducing emissions and meeting climate targets. By decreasing energy consumption, countries can achieve substantial reductions in greenhouse gases without sacrificing economic growth. Efficiency measures complement renewable energy deployment by lowering total energy demand, thus reducing the scale of renewable generation needed to decarbonize systems. Efficiency improvements in energy-intensive industries are particularly critical for achieving net-zero emissions, as they often provide immediate and measurable impacts.

Financing mechanisms and policy frameworks are essential to scaling up energy efficiency. Incentives such as tax credits, low-interest loans, and performance-based grants encourage investment in efficient technologies. Energy service companies (ESCOs) offer models where efficiency upgrades are financed through future energy savings, lowering financial barriers for businesses and public institutions. Regulatory frameworks that establish clear standards and long-term targets create certainty for investors and drive innovation.

Behavioral change complements technological solutions in achieving efficiency goals. Public awareness campaigns, education, and digital feedback tools empower consumers to make informed energy choices. Businesses and households that adopt efficient practices contribute collectively to significant national and global energy savings. Encouraging cultural shifts toward conservation and sustainability reinforces the impact of policy and technological initiatives.

Energy efficiency remains a central pillar of sustainable energy strategies. It enhances competitiveness, reduces emissions, and supports equitable access to affordable energy. Integrating efficiency into planning, investment, and governance ensures that global energy systems evolve toward a more resilient and sustainable future.

Industrial, Building, and Transport Sector Efficiency Measures

Improving energy efficiency across industrial, building, and transport sectors is essential for reducing global energy demand and mitigating environmental impacts. Each sector presents distinct opportunities and challenges that require tailored strategies combining technological innovation, regulatory frameworks, and behavioral change. Efficiency measures in these areas support economic competitiveness, enhance energy security, and contribute to achieving climate and sustainability objectives.

Industrial energy efficiency focuses on optimizing processes, equipment, and resource use in manufacturing and production systems. Industries such as steel, cement, chemicals, and pulp and paper are among the most energy-intensive. Upgrading to high-efficiency machinery, implementing waste heat recovery systems, and adopting cogeneration technologies can significantly reduce energy intensity. The use of sensors, automation, and digital monitoring systems enables precise control of operations and identification of energy-saving opportunities. Circular economy approaches, including material recycling and resource recovery, further enhance efficiency by minimizing waste and extending product lifecycles.

Energy management systems play a critical role in institutionalizing efficiency within industrial operations. Frameworks such as ISO 50001 guide companies in establishing policies, setting performance targets, and continuously improving energy management practices. Integrating efficiency into procurement, maintenance, and production planning ensures long-term energy savings. Industrial clusters and eco-industrial parks can also promote shared infrastructure and resource exchange, reducing overall energy consumption through collaborative efficiency gains.

In the building sector, efficiency measures address both new construction and existing structures. Buildings account for a large share of total energy use, primarily for heating, cooling, lighting, and appliances. Design strategies that emphasize insulation, natural ventilation, and passive solar heating reduce energy demand at minimal cost. High-efficiency HVAC systems, LED lighting, and energy-efficient appliances contribute to significant reductions in operational energy use. Smart building technologies, including automated controls and occupancy sensors, allow dynamic energy management tailored to usage patterns.

Retrofitting existing buildings is a major opportunity for improving efficiency, particularly in urban areas with aging infrastructure. Upgrading insulation, windows, and heating systems reduces energy losses and improves comfort. Building energy codes and performance standards provide regulatory incentives for efficiency upgrades, while energy certification and labeling programs encourage consumer awareness. Urban planning that promotes high-density, mixed-use development reduces transportation energy demand and fosters efficient public service delivery. Integrating renewable energy systems such as rooftop solar further enhances building efficiency and resilience.

In the transport sector, improving energy efficiency reduces emissions and dependence on fossil fuels. Vehicle efficiency standards, fuel economy regulations, and technological innovation in engines and materials have significantly improved the performance of cars, trucks, and aircraft. The transition to electric and hybrid vehicles offers further efficiency gains, especially when powered by renewable energy sources. Lightweight materials, aerodynamic design, and regenerative braking technologies enhance fuel efficiency in road transport.

Public transportation systems contribute to large-scale energy savings by reducing the number of individual vehicles on the road. Expanding and modernizing rail, bus, and metro networks provides efficient mobility options while decreasing congestion and emissions. Promoting non-motorized transport modes, such as cycling and walking, complements these systems and reduces overall energy use. Intelligent transport systems (ITS) supported by digital technologies enable traffic optimization and route planning that minimize fuel consumption.

Freight and logistics present another area for efficiency improvement. Coordinated logistics systems, modal shifts from road to rail or water transport, and optimized supply chains can lower energy intensity in goods movement. Electrification of freight vehicles and the use of alternative fuels such as hydrogen or biofuels offer long-term pathways for decarbonization. Policies that promote fleet renewal and emission standards further encourage adoption of efficient technologies.

Cross-sectoral approaches enhance the overall impact of efficiency measures. Coordinating policies among industry, building, and transport sectors ensures consistency and maximizes benefits across the energy system. Investment in research, innovation, and skills development supports the diffusion of advanced technologies and sustainable practices. International cooperation and knowledge sharing accelerate progress, enabling countries to adopt proven strategies suited to their specific development and resource contexts.

Behavioral and Technological Innovation for Efficiency Gains

Behavioral and technological innovations play complementary roles in improving energy efficiency across all sectors. While technology provides the tools and systems to reduce energy consumption, behavioral change ensures that these tools are used effectively and consistently. Together, they drive long-term reductions in energy demand and support the transition toward sustainable energy systems.

Behavioral change focuses on modifying consumption patterns and decision-making processes among individuals, households, and organizations. Public awareness campaigns, education programs, and incentives can encourage more responsible energy use. Simple actions, such as turning off unused lights, managing heating and cooling settings, or maintaining appliances properly, yield measurable energy savings when adopted widely. Behavioral insights, including feedback mechanisms and social comparisons, have proven effective in motivating consumers to adopt energy-efficient habits.

Institutional behavior also shapes energy outcomes. Businesses, government agencies, and public institutions influence efficiency through procurement policies, facility management, and operational practices. Adopting internal energy management systems and employee engagement programs fosters a culture of efficiency. Providing feedback on energy performance and recognizing achievements encourages sustained participation. Behavioral initiatives are most successful when supported by clear information, financial incentives, and visible leadership commitment.

Technological innovation underpins efficiency improvements by transforming how energy is produced, distributed, and consumed. Advances in energy-efficient equipment, digitalization, and smart technologies allow for greater control, optimization, and monitoring of energy systems. High-efficiency motors, variable-speed drives, and advanced control systems reduce industrial energy intensity. In buildings, technologies such as smart thermostats, automated lighting, and intelligent metering systems optimize energy use according to real-time occupancy and environmental conditions.

Digital transformation enhances energy efficiency through data-driven decision-making. The integration of artificial intelligence, machine learning, and the Internet of Things (IoT) enables continuous analysis of energy consumption patterns. Predictive analytics identify inefficiencies, allowing timely interventions. Smart grids coordinate electricity supply and demand dynamically, reducing losses and improving system reliability. These technologies support both consumers and utilities in managing energy more efficiently and flexibly.

Energy-efficient product innovation contributes significantly to demand reduction. Appliance standards and labeling programs encourage manufacturers to design products that meet higher efficiency thresholds. Advances in materials science, such as improved insulation, low-emission glass, and lightweight composites, enhance the performance of buildings and vehicles. Industrial innovation focuses on process redesign, waste heat recovery, and resource optimization. Technological progress also enables the development of cleaner production methods, minimizing emissions while conserving energy.

The combination of behavior and technology delivers greater efficiency than either approach alone. For example, automated systems can reduce energy use, but their effectiveness depends on user engagement and correct operation. Similarly, technological potential can be undermined by habits or institutional inertia that prevent optimal use. Policies and programs that integrate both behavioral and technological dimensions can achieve sustained improvements in energy performance.

Governments play a key role in fostering innovation and behavior change through policy design and regulation. Efficiency standards, financial incentives, and research funding accelerate technological deployment. Public information campaigns, energy audits, and community-based initiatives raise awareness and build capacity. Behavioral economics tools, such as nudges and default settings, help encourage energy-saving choices without restricting freedom of choice.

Private sector innovation drives efficiency through research, competition, and market transformation. Companies that invest in efficient technologies gain advantages through cost savings and improved sustainability performance. Collaboration between public institutions, research organizations, and industry accelerates the diffusion of new technologies and best practices. Start-ups and energy service companies (ESCOs) play an important role in bringing tailored solutions to consumers and businesses.

Behavioral and technological innovations are interconnected forces shaping the evolution of energy systems. Together, they enable continuous improvement, reduce consumption, and foster a culture of efficiency that supports economic and environmental sustainability.

Energy Efficiency and the Circular Economy

Energy efficiency and the circular economy are mutually reinforcing concepts that promote sustainable resource use and reduce environmental impact. While energy efficiency focuses on minimizing energy consumption through improved technologies and practices, the circular economy emphasizes keeping materials and products in use for as long as possible. Integrating both approaches enables societies to achieve deeper decarbonization, lower resource dependency, and greater economic resilience.

The linear model of production and consumption, based on extract-use-dispose patterns, leads to high energy demand and significant waste generation. Each stage of this model—resource extraction, manufacturing, transport, use, and disposal—requires substantial energy inputs. Transitioning to a circular model reduces these energy requirements by promoting reuse, repair, remanufacturing, and recycling. By extending product lifecycles and designing systems that minimize waste, circular economy practices directly contribute to reducing overall energy intensity across industries.

Industrial systems present major opportunities to combine energy efficiency with circular principles. Resource recovery and industrial symbiosis—where waste or by-products from one process become inputs for another—can reduce both material and energy use. For example, utilizing waste heat from manufacturing processes or converting organic waste into biogas enhances efficiency while supporting circularity. Process optimization and digital monitoring further enable energy savings by identifying inefficiencies and opportunities for material reuse. Integrating circular economy strategies into industrial planning supports competitiveness and lowers dependence on virgin resources.

Product design is a critical link between energy efficiency and circularity. Designing products for durability, modularity, and recyclability reduces the energy required for manufacturing new goods. Materials with lower embodied energy and improved recyclability help decrease lifecycle energy consumption. Incorporating energy-efficient components, such as low-power electronics and lightweight materials, further enhances performance while reducing environmental impact. Policies that encourage eco-design standards and extended producer responsibility strengthen the connection between efficiency and circular innovation.

In the building sector, circular economy principles complement energy efficiency by promoting adaptive reuse, modular construction, and material recovery. Energy-efficient design reduces operational energy demand, while circular practices minimize embodied energy through recycling and reuse of construction materials. Retrofitting existing buildings to improve insulation, lighting, and heating systems avoids the high energy costs associated with demolition and new construction. Using locally sourced and recycled materials in construction further supports both energy efficiency and circular resource management.

The energy sector itself can adopt circular approaches to enhance efficiency. Renewable energy technologies, such as wind turbines and solar panels, require materials that can be reused or recycled at the end of their lifespan. Developing closed-loop systems for energy technologies ensures that valuable materials are recovered and reintegrated into production cycles. Additionally, the use of bioenergy and waste-to-energy systems can turn residual waste streams into useful energy sources, reducing pressure on landfills while providing renewable alternatives to fossil fuels.

Digitalization facilitates the convergence of energy efficiency and the circular economy. Smart technologies enable tracking of energy and material flows across value chains, improving transparency and optimization. Data analytics help businesses identify opportunities for resource efficiency, predictive maintenance, and waste reduction. Platforms that support product sharing, leasing, and remanufacturing extend product lifetimes and reduce the energy required for new production. Digital solutions empower consumers to make informed choices, further supporting energy-efficient and circular consumption patterns.

Policy frameworks are essential for integrating energy efficiency and circular economy strategies. Governments can align regulatory instruments such as efficiency standards, waste reduction targets, and green public procurement to promote synergies between both agendas. Financial incentives, tax reforms, and innovation funding encourage businesses to adopt circular and efficient practices. International collaboration facilitates the exchange of technologies and best practices, helping economies scale up integrated solutions that reduce energy and resource use simultaneously.

The alignment of energy efficiency with circular economy principles transforms how societies use resources, design systems, and create value. It supports economic growth while minimizing energy demand and environmental pressures through systemic, interconnected approaches that close resource loops and optimize energy performance.

Chapter 4: Renewable Energy Transitions and Energy Security

The transition to renewable energy is reshaping the foundation of global energy security. Expanding the use of solar, wind, hydropower, and other renewable sources reduces dependence on fossil fuels, diversifies supply, and enhances resilience against market volatility and geopolitical risks. Renewable systems also offer environmental benefits by cutting emissions and promoting cleaner production and consumption patterns. However, this transformation presents new challenges, including the integration of variable energy sources, investment in grid modernization, and the sustainable management of critical materials. This chapter examines how renewable energy transitions can strengthen long-term energy security while supporting global sustainability goals.

The Strategic Role of Renewable Energy in Energy Security

Renewable energy plays a central role in strengthening energy security by diversifying energy sources, reducing dependence on imports, and mitigating exposure to price volatility. As global energy demand rises and fossil fuel resources become increasingly constrained, renewable energy offers a sustainable pathway to meet long-term needs. Technologies such as solar, wind, hydropower, geothermal, and biomass contribute to reliable, resilient, and low-carbon energy systems capable of supporting economic growth while addressing environmental challenges.

Diversification is a key principle of energy security, and renewable energy enhances this by expanding the range of available energy sources. Countries heavily reliant on imported fossil fuels face risks from supply disruptions, geopolitical tensions, and fluctuating prices. By integrating renewables into national energy mixes, these countries can reduce vulnerability to external shocks and improve self-sufficiency. Renewable resources are often locally available, allowing nations to generate power domestically and retain economic benefits within their borders. This decentralization of production also reduces the risk of widespread outages and enhances system resilience.

Renewable energy contributes to price stability by reducing exposure to volatile fossil fuel markets. The marginal cost of renewable generation is low once infrastructure is established, as sunlight, wind, and water are not subject to market fluctuations. This creates more predictable electricity prices and shields economies from sudden increases in fuel costs. In the long term, renewables help stabilize energy expenditures for both consumers and industries, supporting economic planning and competitiveness.

Technological innovation has been instrumental in making renewable energy a strategic component of energy security. Advances in energy storage, grid management, and forecasting have improved the reliability and integration of variable sources such as solar and wind. Battery storage systems and pumped hydropower balance supply and demand, ensuring stable power delivery even when renewable generation fluctuates. Smart grids and digital monitoring enhance flexibility and efficiency, allowing renewable energy to complement conventional sources within diversified power systems.

Energy independence through renewable deployment strengthens national security by reducing reliance on imported fuels. This independence provides governments with greater control over energy policy and reduces exposure to global supply chain disruptions. In regions affected by conflict or political instability, renewable systems—particularly decentralized models like microgrids and off-grid solar—ensure continuity of essential services. This resilience supports social stability and economic recovery, particularly in remote or disaster-prone areas.

The environmental benefits of renewable energy align closely with long-term energy security. Fossil fuel-based systems contribute to air pollution, resource depletion, and climate change, all of which undermine the reliability of energy supply. Extreme weather events, droughts, and heatwaves increasingly disrupt conventional energy infrastructure. By contrast, renewables reduce greenhouse gas emissions and reliance on water-intensive energy processes, contributing to environmental stability. A stable climate supports the long-term availability of natural resources critical for energy production.

Economic development and job creation are additional dimensions of renewable energy's contribution to energy security. Expanding renewable industries stimulates domestic manufacturing, installation, and maintenance services. Localized supply chains enhance energy sovereignty and create employment opportunities across skill levels. Training programs and education initiatives support the development of a skilled workforce capable of maintaining and expanding renewable systems. These socioeconomic benefits strengthen national resilience and reduce dependence on global energy markets.

Regional cooperation on renewable energy infrastructure further enhances energy security. Cross-border electricity interconnections, shared research initiatives, and joint investment frameworks promote resource optimization and technological innovation. Regions with abundant renewable potential can export clean energy to neighboring markets, diversifying income sources and stabilizing regional power systems. International collaboration also supports standardization, financing, and technology transfer, enabling faster deployment of renewables globally.

Financing mechanisms play a crucial role in scaling renewable energy deployment. Stable policy environments, transparent regulations, and risk mitigation instruments attract investment from both public and private sectors. Instruments such as green bonds, power purchase agreements, and feed-in tariffs create predictable returns and facilitate long-term project development. International financial institutions and climate funds provide additional support, helping developing countries overcome barriers to adoption and strengthen energy security through renewable integration.

Integrating renewable energy into national energy strategies requires coordinated planning and governance. Policymakers must ensure that renewable deployment aligns with grid capacity, market structures, and regulatory frameworks. Investment in infrastructure, such as transmission networks and energy storage, enhances system reliability. Transparent and adaptive governance mechanisms encourage innovation while maintaining stability in energy markets.

Renewable energy's strategic role extends beyond energy supply to encompass economic, environmental, and social dimensions of security. It enables diversification, resilience, and sustainability in an increasingly uncertain global energy landscape, forming a foundation for stable and self-reliant energy systems.

Integration of Variable Renewables into Power Systems

Integrating variable renewable energy sources such as solar and wind into power systems presents both opportunities and challenges. These technologies are key to decarbonizing electricity generation but their variability and intermittency require careful management to maintain system reliability and stability. Effective integration involves technological innovation, grid modernization, regulatory adaptation, and investment in flexibility measures that allow renewable energy to operate harmoniously with conventional power systems.

Variable renewables differ from traditional energy sources because their output depends on weather conditions and time of day. Solar power generation peaks during daylight hours and declines at night, while wind power fluctuates with wind speed and patterns. These variations create imbalances between supply and demand if not properly managed. Integrating such sources requires enhancing grid flexibility through storage, demand response, and diversified generation portfolios. Predictive modeling and improved forecasting techniques help grid operators anticipate fluctuations and adjust system operations in real time.

Energy storage plays a central role in integrating variable renewables. Technologies such as lithium-ion batteries, pumped hydro, and emerging long-duration storage systems enable excess energy to be stored when production exceeds demand and released when generation declines. This helps smooth out short-term fluctuations and maintain grid stability. Storage also supports ancillary services such as frequency regulation and voltage control, ensuring consistent power quality. Expanding storage capacity through targeted investment and innovation enhances system resilience and allows greater renewable penetration.

Grid modernization is essential for accommodating variable renewable energy. Traditional power grids were designed for centralized, predictable generation, while renewable energy often comes from decentralized and distributed sources. Upgrading transmission and distribution infrastructure improves the capacity to transport renewable electricity from resource-rich areas to demand centers. Smart grid technologies enable real-time monitoring, two-way communication, and automated control, improving efficiency and responsiveness. Digital platforms and data analytics enhance grid visibility, allowing for faster detection of disturbances and more efficient system balancing.

Diversification of renewable energy sources reduces the overall variability of supply. Combining solar, wind, hydro, and geothermal energy across different regions and timeframes creates complementary generation patterns. Geographic dispersion of renewable projects minimizes the impact of local weather fluctuations and reduces the need for large-scale curtailment. Interconnected regional grids further enhance flexibility by enabling electricity exchange between areas with differing generation and demand profiles. Coordinated planning across jurisdictions supports optimal use of renewable resources and infrastructure.

Demand-side management provides additional flexibility in balancing supply and demand. By encouraging consumers to adjust energy use in response to price signals or grid conditions, demand response programs reduce peak loads and improve system efficiency. Smart meters and automated control systems allow for dynamic adjustments in electricity consumption, aligning demand with renewable generation patterns. Integrating demand-side flexibility into market structures incentivizes participation and supports overall system reliability.

Policy and market reforms are necessary to support the integration of variable renewables. Traditional regulatory frameworks often favor conventional generation models that do not account for the unique characteristics of renewable energy. Modernized electricity markets that value flexibility, ancillary services, and distributed generation encourage investment in technologies that complement renewables. Transparent pricing mechanisms and long-term contracts provide financial stability for renewable projects while supporting competition and innovation.

Investment in research and development continues to improve integration strategies. Advances in power electronics, grid-forming inverters, and hybrid systems enhance the ability of renewables to contribute to grid stability. Emerging digital technologies, including artificial intelligence and machine learning, optimize forecasting, scheduling, and maintenance. International collaboration and standardization accelerate the adoption of best practices and technical solutions that facilitate high shares of renewables.

Capacity building and institutional coordination are critical for successful integration. Training grid operators, planners, and policymakers ensures that technical, regulatory, and operational frameworks evolve in line with renewable expansion. Collaboration among utilities, regulators, and technology providers strengthens resilience and adaptability in managing complex power systems.

The integration of variable renewables into power systems requires a coordinated approach that combines technology, policy, and market innovation. Expanding flexibility, modernizing infrastructure, and enhancing coordination enable renewable energy to become a stable and reliable foundation of future electricity systems.

Storage, Smart Grids, and Digitalization

Energy storage, smart grids, and digitalization are transforming power systems by enhancing flexibility, reliability, and efficiency. As renewable energy becomes a larger share of the energy mix, these technologies play a crucial role in managing variability, balancing supply and demand, and ensuring stable electricity delivery. Their integration supports the transition to decentralized, low-carbon energy systems that can adapt to changing consumption patterns and market conditions.

Energy storage provides a critical buffer between energy generation and consumption. Technologies such as batteries, pumped hydro, compressed air, and thermal storage allow surplus electricity to be stored during periods of low demand and released when demand is high. This helps stabilize grid operations and reduces the need for fossil fuel-based backup generation. Short-term storage solutions, such as lithium-ion batteries, are well suited for frequency regulation and load shifting, while long-duration storage technologies provide seasonal flexibility and resilience against extended renewable shortfalls. Expanding energy storage capacity enables higher shares of renewables to be integrated without compromising reliability.

Smart grids represent a modernization of traditional electricity networks through the application of advanced communication and control technologies. They enable real-time monitoring of electricity flows, automated fault detection, and dynamic load management. Smart grids integrate distributed energy resources such as rooftop solar, electric vehicles, and battery systems into the network, enhancing flexibility and efficiency. Two-way communication between utilities and consumers allows for more responsive demand-side management, reducing peak loads and optimizing energy distribution. Smart grids also facilitate microgrid development, enabling localized resilience and community-based energy management.

Digitalization is central to the operation and optimization of modern energy systems. Digital tools such as sensors, data analytics, artificial intelligence, and machine learning provide insights into system performance and user behavior. These technologies allow grid operators to forecast renewable generation, predict maintenance needs, and manage assets more efficiently. Data-driven decision-making improves system reliability, reduces operational costs, and enhances planning for infrastructure investment. Digital platforms also enable new business models, including peer-to-peer energy trading and virtual power plants that aggregate distributed resources into coordinated networks.

Energy storage and digitalization complement each other in improving grid management. Smart control systems coordinate storage deployment based on real-time data, maximizing system efficiency. Predictive algorithms optimize when to charge or discharge storage assets, taking into account electricity prices, weather forecasts, and demand patterns. By integrating storage with digitalized grid management, utilities can enhance flexibility, minimize curtailment of renewable energy, and respond quickly to fluctuations in supply or demand.

Cybersecurity is an emerging priority as energy systems become increasingly digital and interconnected. Protecting networks from cyber threats requires robust data protection protocols, continuous monitoring, and coordinated response mechanisms. Regulatory frameworks and industry standards are evolving to ensure that digital infrastructure remains secure and resilient against potential disruptions.

The widespread deployment of smart meters and digital interfaces empowers consumers to participate actively in energy management. Real-time information on consumption patterns enables households and businesses to adjust usage based on price signals or grid conditions. Demand response programs, supported by digital communication, allow consumers to reduce or shift energy use during peak periods, contributing to overall system efficiency. This participatory approach fosters greater engagement and awareness of energy sustainability.

Policy and regulation play a crucial role in accelerating the deployment of storage, smart grids, and digital technologies. Governments can encourage innovation through research funding, pilot projects, and standardization initiatives. Market reforms that value flexibility and ancillary services create incentives for investment in these technologies. Collaboration among utilities, technology developers, and consumers is necessary to ensure interoperability and equitable access to the benefits of digital transformation.

The integration of storage, smart grids, and digitalization is reshaping power systems into more adaptive, efficient, and sustainable networks. Together, they enable higher renewable energy penetration, improved reliability, and greater consumer participation in the evolving energy landscape.

Socioeconomic Co-Benefits and Challenges of Renewable Expansion

The expansion of renewable energy delivers wide-ranging socioeconomic benefits, including job creation, economic diversification, public health improvements, and enhanced social equity. At the same time, it introduces challenges related to workforce transitions, land use, infrastructure needs, and policy coordination. Maximizing the benefits of renewable energy while managing its associated risks requires inclusive planning, investment in skills development, and equitable policy design.

Renewable energy industries contribute significantly to job creation across manufacturing, installation, maintenance, and research sectors. Solar and wind technologies are particularly labor-intensive during construction and installation phases, generating employment opportunities at local and national levels. Jobs in renewable energy tend to be more geographically distributed than those in fossil fuel industries, providing economic opportunities in rural and remote areas. As the sector grows, workforce training and education become essential to ensure workers possess the technical skills required for operation and maintenance of new technologies.

Economic diversification is another key benefit of renewable energy expansion. By reducing dependence on imported fossil fuels, countries can stabilize trade balances and strengthen energy independence. Domestic renewable industries stimulate innovation, attract investment, and create new markets for goods and services. Developing renewable energy supply chains—ranging from component manufacturing to logistics and data management—supports industrial growth and fosters entrepreneurship. Local manufacturing and service provision also retain a larger share of economic value within national economies.

Public health benefits arise from the reduction of air pollution associated with fossil fuel combustion. Cleaner energy sources decrease exposure to harmful particulates, leading to fewer respiratory and cardiovascular diseases. These improvements translate into reduced healthcare costs and higher productivity. Renewable energy systems also minimize the risk of environmental accidents such as oil spills or methane leaks, contributing to safer and more sustainable living conditions. Improved air quality enhances quality of life, particularly in densely populated urban centers where pollution levels are often high.

Access to affordable and reliable renewable energy can strengthen social inclusion and equity. Off-grid and mini-grid renewable systems expand access to electricity in regions that lack grid infrastructure, supporting education, healthcare, and economic activities. These systems enable rural communities to participate in modern economies and improve livelihoods through productive uses of energy. Gender equity also improves when clean energy reduces reliance on traditional biomass for cooking and heating, lessening health risks and freeing time for education and income generation.

Despite these benefits, renewable energy expansion introduces several socioeconomic challenges. Workforce transitions present one of the most pressing issues. As economies shift away from fossil fuels, workers in coal, oil, and gas sectors may face job losses or relocation. Managing these transitions requires comprehensive retraining programs, income support, and regional diversification strategies to ensure that affected communities share in the benefits of the clean energy transition. Social dialogue between governments, businesses, and labor organizations is vital to achieving a fair and inclusive transition.

Land use and resource management are additional challenges associated with large-scale renewable deployment. Solar farms, wind parks, and bioenergy crops require substantial land areas, which can create competition with agriculture, conservation, or residential use. Transparent land-use planning and community consultation help mitigate conflicts and ensure that local populations benefit from renewable projects. Environmental assessments and biodiversity protection measures maintain ecological integrity while supporting energy development.

Infrastructure and investment requirements can also pose constraints, particularly in developing economies. Expanding renewable generation necessitates upgrades to transmission networks, storage systems, and grid management capabilities. Mobilizing finance for these investments often depends on stable policy environments and clear regulatory frameworks. Governments must balance public investment with incentives that attract private sector participation, ensuring equitable access to the benefits of renewable expansion.

Policy coordination is essential to align renewable energy development with broader economic and social goals. Well-designed policies integrate energy, labor, and environmental objectives to maximize co-benefits while addressing challenges. Education and vocational training initiatives prepare the workforce for emerging opportunities in clean energy industries. Local content requirements and innovation policies stimulate domestic value creation and technological progress.

Renewable energy expansion has the potential to deliver significant socioeconomic gains, but achieving these outcomes requires inclusive and adaptive governance. By addressing workforce, land, and infrastructure challenges, countries can ensure that the transition to renewables supports sustainable growth, social stability, and long-term prosperity.

Chapter 5: Fossil Fuels, Just Transition, and Sustainable Development

Fossil fuels remain integral to the global energy mix, providing the foundation for industrialization, mobility, and economic growth. Yet their continued use poses significant environmental and social challenges, particularly in meeting global climate objectives and reducing emissions. Managing the gradual decline of fossil fuel dependence requires careful planning to protect workers, communities, and economies reliant on these industries. A just transition emphasizes fairness, inclusivity, and opportunity in this process, ensuring that the move toward low-carbon systems supports social stability and sustainable livelihoods. This chapter explores how fossil fuels can be phased down responsibly within the broader framework of sustainable development.

The Continuing Role of Fossil Fuels in Global Energy Systems

Fossil fuels continue to play a dominant role in global energy systems despite accelerating efforts to decarbonize the economy. Coal, oil, and natural gas collectively supply the majority of the world's energy, supporting industrial production, transportation, electricity generation, and heating. Their prevalence is due to established infrastructure, high energy density, and decades of technological investment. While renewable energy is expanding rapidly, the scale and inertia of existing systems ensure that fossil fuels will remain part of the energy landscape for the foreseeable future.

Coal has historically been the backbone of electricity generation and industrial development. Its abundance and low cost have made it a key source of power, particularly in emerging economies undergoing rapid industrialization. However, coal combustion is the most carbon-intensive form of energy use, and many countries are phasing down its role to meet climate targets. Modernization of coal plants through efficiency improvements and emissions control technologies can reduce environmental impact in the short term, but long-term reliance on coal remains incompatible with global climate objectives. Transition strategies increasingly focus on accelerating the retirement of coal assets while supporting affected workers and regions.

Oil remains the primary fuel for global transportation and an important feedstock for petrochemical industries. The mobility sector's dependence on oil reflects the widespread use of internal combustion engines and the established global supply chain for refining and distribution. Despite growing adoption of electric vehicles and alternative fuels, demand for oil persists in aviation, shipping, and heavy transport, where electrification is progressing more slowly. The petrochemical industry continues to rely on oil derivatives for plastics, fertilizers, and other materials. Over time, efficiency improvements, biofuels, and circular economy practices may reduce oil demand, but complete substitution will require significant technological and infrastructural transformation.

Natural gas has gained prominence as a transitional fuel in the shift toward lower-carbon energy systems. It produces fewer emissions than coal and oil when used for power generation or heating and can complement intermittent renewable sources by providing flexible backup capacity. Many countries have invested heavily in gas infrastructure, including pipelines and liquefied natural gas (LNG) terminals, to enhance energy security and diversification. However, methane leakage throughout the gas supply chain presents a significant challenge, as it undermines the climate benefits of gas relative to other fossil fuels. Reducing leakage through improved monitoring and stricter regulation is essential to maintaining gas's role as a bridge fuel.

The economic and geopolitical dimensions of fossil fuels continue to shape global energy systems. Energy-exporting countries depend heavily on fossil fuel revenues to support public finances, employment, and economic growth. Sharp declines in demand could destabilize these economies without adequate diversification strategies. Conversely, importing countries remain vulnerable to supply disruptions and price volatility driven by geopolitical tensions or production cuts. Energy security considerations therefore continue to influence the pace and direction of the global energy transition. Policymakers face the challenge of balancing decarbonization with stability in global energy markets.

Technological innovation has improved the efficiency and environmental performance of fossil fuel use. Carbon capture, utilization, and storage (CCUS) technologies offer the potential to mitigate emissions from industrial processes and power generation. While deployment remains limited due to high costs and infrastructure requirements, CCUS could play a role in achieving net-zero targets, particularly in hard-to-abate sectors such as cement, steel, and chemicals. Advances in cleaner fuel production, such as hydrogen derived from natural gas with carbon capture, provide additional pathways to reduce emissions while leveraging existing fossil infrastructure.

Fossil fuel investment patterns are evolving as investors increasingly account for climate risk, policy changes, and social expectations. Financial institutions are tightening lending criteria for high-emission projects, while companies are diversifying into renewables, hydrogen, and carbon management technologies. Despite this shift, fossil fuel investments continue in regions where energy demand is growing rapidly and alternatives remain limited. Ensuring that new projects align with long-term sustainability goals requires transparent governance, environmental safeguards, and integration with national energy transition strategies.

The phase-down of fossil fuels must consider social and economic implications. Many regions depend on fossil fuel industries for employment and local development. Abrupt transitions risk creating economic dislocation and social unrest. Just transition frameworks aim to manage these impacts through retraining programs, social protection, and regional development initiatives. International cooperation can support fossil fuel-dependent economies by facilitating technology transfer, investment in clean industries, and diversification of revenue sources.

Fossil fuels will continue to play a role in global energy systems during the transition to sustainable energy. Their continued use highlights the complexity of balancing economic growth, energy security, and environmental goals. Managing this transition effectively requires gradual but decisive policy action, technological innovation, and equitable solutions that support both producers and consumers in the evolving global energy landscape.

Managing Decline: Coal Phase-Outs and Transition Policies

Phasing out coal represents one of the most significant challenges in achieving global decarbonization while maintaining energy security and economic stability. Coal has long been a foundational energy source for power generation and industrial production, but its high carbon intensity makes it incompatible with long-term climate objectives. Managing its decline requires coordinated policies that balance environmental goals with economic and social considerations, ensuring that affected regions and workers are supported through the transition.

Coal phase-outs are being driven by a combination of environmental regulation, market dynamics, and technological change. Stricter emission standards, carbon pricing mechanisms, and commitments under international climate agreements have reduced the competitiveness of coal compared to cleaner alternatives. At the same time, the rapid decline in renewable energy costs has accelerated the shift toward solar, wind, and natural gas. In many regions, renewable power combined with storage now provides a more cost-effective and reliable option than new or existing coal plants. These market trends have led to early plant retirements and declining investment in new coal capacity.

Transition policies play a critical role in ensuring that coal phase-outs occur in a planned and equitable manner. Governments must establish clear timelines and regulatory frameworks that provide certainty for investors and stakeholders. Gradual and predictable phase-out schedules allow utilities and industries to adjust operations, manage stranded assets, and reallocate capital to cleaner energy sources. Policy instruments such as emissions trading systems, renewable energy mandates, and investment incentives help align market behavior with long-term decarbonization targets. Effective transition strategies integrate energy, labor, and regional development policies to minimize disruption.

Economic diversification is central to managing the decline of coal-dependent regions. Communities built around mining and power generation often rely heavily on coal for employment and local revenue. As coal activities wind down, investments in alternative industries—such as renewable energy, advanced manufacturing, or sustainable agriculture—create new sources of income and economic opportunity. Infrastructure development, innovation hubs, and public–private partnerships support this diversification by attracting new businesses and encouraging entrepreneurship. Regional transition funds financed through carbon revenues or public budgets can provide targeted financial assistance for redevelopment projects.

Workforce transition measures are essential to mitigate the social impacts of coal phase-outs. Workers in mining, transport, and power generation require retraining and reskilling to adapt to new sectors. Education and vocational training programs, supported by public funding and industry collaboration, prepare employees for emerging opportunities in renewable energy, energy efficiency, and environmental restoration. Social protection measures such as wage subsidies, pension support, and relocation assistance ensure a just transition that prioritizes the well-being of affected workers and their families.

Repurposing existing coal infrastructure can reduce transition costs and provide continued value to local economies. Decommissioned coal plants can be converted into renewable energy hubs, industrial parks, or energy storage facilities. Mine sites offer potential for land reclamation, ecological restoration, or the development of new industries such as tourism and sustainable construction materials. These initiatives not only create employment but also restore environmental integrity in regions affected by decades of extraction.

International cooperation supports coal phase-out efforts through financial and technical assistance. Multilateral development banks and climate finance institutions provide funding for clean energy investments and economic diversification programs. Initiatives such as the Just Energy Transition Partnerships (JETPs) mobilize international resources to help coal-dependent countries transition toward low-carbon energy systems. Knowledge exchange, capacity building, and technology transfer enhance the ability of developing economies to implement effective transition policies aligned with their national development priorities.

Managing the decline of coal requires transparent governance and inclusive stakeholder engagement. Engaging workers, local governments, industry, and civil society in planning processes builds trust and ensures that transition policies reflect shared objectives. Clear communication about timelines, policy measures, and expected outcomes helps maintain public support. Coordinated planning across energy, labor, and environmental ministries ensures that the transition is coherent and sustainable.

The phase-out of coal is an inevitable component of global climate policy. A managed transition guided by sound policies, economic diversification, and social inclusion can reduce disruption, promote fairness, and create opportunities for long-term sustainable growth.

Ensuring a Just Transition for Workers and Communities

A just transition ensures that the shift toward low-carbon energy systems does not leave workers and communities behind. As economies move away from fossil fuel dependence, policies must address the social and economic impacts on those whose livelihoods rely on carbon-intensive industries. A fair transition balances climate objectives with employment protection, social equity, and regional development, creating pathways for sustainable and inclusive growth.

The energy transition affects workers across coal, oil, and gas industries, as well as associated sectors such as transport and heavy manufacturing. Job losses, declining local revenues, and reduced economic activity can create significant social challenges in regions reliant on fossil fuels. A just transition framework anticipates these disruptions through proactive planning, investment, and social dialogue. Policies should be designed to protect incomes, retrain workers, and create new employment opportunities in emerging industries such as renewable energy, energy efficiency, and environmental rehabilitation.

Workforce reskilling and retraining programs are central to just transition strategies. As fossil fuel industries decline, workers need support to transition into new roles requiring different skills. Governments, educational institutions, and private companies can collaborate to develop training programs aligned with future labor market demands. Technical and vocational education focused on renewable energy installation, maintenance, and manufacturing enables workers to participate in the growing clean energy economy. Lifelong learning initiatives ensure adaptability as technologies and market needs evolve. Financial assistance for education and relocation supports workers through the adjustment period.

Social protection systems provide security for workers and families during the transition. Measures such as unemployment benefits, wage insurance, pension protection, and healthcare access mitigate financial hardship. Targeted social assistance for vulnerable groups, including older workers and those in remote communities, ensures that the benefits of the energy transition are shared equitably. Public employment programs and community-based projects can provide interim job opportunities while long-term economic diversification takes shape.

Community engagement and participation are vital to building trust and ownership in the transition process. Affected communities must be involved in decision-making from the outset to ensure that policies reflect local priorities and needs. Consultation mechanisms, regional transition councils, and participatory planning processes create platforms for collaboration between government, industry, labor unions, and civil society. Transparent communication about the pace and scope of change helps manage expectations and reduce resistance to reform.

Economic diversification supports long-term community resilience. Coal- and oil-dependent regions can attract new industries through strategic investment in infrastructure, technology, and innovation. Developing renewable energy projects, sustainable agriculture, tourism, or advanced manufacturing provides alternative sources of income and employment. Local content requirements and incentives for small and medium-sized enterprises encourage regional entrepreneurship and economic self-sufficiency. Public–private partnerships and regional development funds can finance infrastructure upgrades, industrial clusters, and business incubators that stimulate new economic activity.

Environmental restoration and land rehabilitation create additional employment opportunities while improving local ecosystems. Reclaiming former mining areas, restoring soil and water quality, and developing green spaces contribute to environmental recovery and public health. These projects can employ displaced workers and foster community pride by transforming degraded landscapes into productive or recreational areas. Integrating environmental objectives into transition planning ensures that economic and ecological benefits align.

International cooperation enhances national efforts to ensure a just transition. Multilateral organizations, development banks, and climate finance mechanisms provide technical assistance and funding for social and economic restructuring. Initiatives that promote knowledge exchange and capacity building enable countries to learn from successful transition models. Cross-border partnerships can support regional development strategies that diversify economies and strengthen social resilience.

A just transition requires coherent policy coordination across energy, labor, education, and social ministries. Governments must align climate and employment policies, ensuring that emissions reduction targets are matched with measures to protect and empower workers and communities. Long-term planning supported by transparent governance and adequate financing provides stability and confidence during structural change. Effective implementation transforms potential disruption into opportunity, enabling inclusive participation in the low-carbon economy.

Balancing Energy Security with Climate Commitments

Balancing energy security with climate commitments is one of the most complex challenges facing governments and industries during the global energy transition. Reliable access to affordable energy underpins economic stability and social welfare, while climate commitments require a rapid reduction in greenhouse gas emissions. Achieving both objectives demands integrated policy frameworks that ensure continuity of supply, manage economic risks, and accelerate the shift toward cleaner energy sources.

Energy security depends on the availability, affordability, and resilience of energy systems. Countries must maintain sufficient capacity to meet demand while minimizing exposure to supply disruptions, price volatility, and geopolitical tensions. Traditionally, fossil fuels have provided this stability due to established infrastructure and predictable supply chains. However, their continued use contributes significantly to global emissions, creating a tension between short-term reliability and long-term sustainability. The transition toward low-carbon energy systems must therefore be managed in a way that maintains system stability while reducing emissions intensity.

Climate commitments, anchored in international frameworks such as the Paris Agreement, require countries to decarbonize their economies through renewable energy deployment, energy efficiency, and carbon pricing. Meeting these commitments involves restructuring entire energy systems and industries. Rapid decarbonization without careful planning, however, can create vulnerabilities such as energy shortages, high costs, or social inequities. Policymakers must coordinate climate strategies with national energy security goals to ensure that decarbonization proceeds without compromising reliability or access.

Diversification of energy sources is a key strategy for balancing these objectives. Expanding renewable energy portfolios through solar, wind, hydro, and geothermal power reduces dependence on imported fossil fuels while enhancing domestic energy resilience. Incorporating flexible generation sources such as natural gas and bioenergy can provide stability as renewable capacity expands. Hybrid systems that integrate renewables with energy storage or hydrogen improve grid flexibility and supply continuity. Diversification across geographic regions also mitigates the risks associated with localized weather or resource fluctuations.

Investment in energy infrastructure underpins both energy security and climate goals. Upgrading transmission networks, expanding interconnections, and deploying smart grid technologies enable more efficient integration of renewable energy. Enhancing energy storage capacity ensures stability during periods of variable generation. Modernizing infrastructure also reduces technical losses and improves the resilience of systems to physical and cyber threats. Infrastructure investment must align with long-term sustainability objectives to avoid locking in high-emission assets that could become stranded as climate policies tighten.

Energy efficiency measures complement supply-side strategies by reducing overall demand and easing pressure on energy systems. Improved efficiency in buildings, industry, and transport reduces fuel consumption and emissions while lowering costs for consumers. Demand-side management programs that encourage flexible consumption patterns can help balance intermittent renewable generation. By lowering peak demand, efficiency measures enhance system reliability and free resources for other economic priorities.

Policy coherence is essential for balancing climate and security objectives. Governments must integrate energy, climate, and industrial policies to ensure consistent direction and avoid counterproductive measures. Carbon pricing, subsidy reform, and targeted incentives create signals that encourage clean energy investment while maintaining affordability. Long-term planning, supported by transparent regulatory frameworks, allows investors and utilities to manage risks effectively. Policy stability and predictability are critical to sustaining progress in both energy security and decarbonization.

International cooperation strengthens the alignment between energy security and climate commitments. Cross-border electricity trade, regional infrastructure development, and shared research initiatives enhance resource efficiency and system resilience. Collaboration on clean energy technologies, such as hydrogen and carbon capture, accelerates innovation and reduces costs. Financial and technical support from international organizations helps developing countries pursue low-carbon transitions while maintaining secure access to energy.

Social and economic factors also influence the balance between energy security and climate objectives. Energy affordability is vital to prevent inequities during the transition. Policies must protect vulnerable populations from price volatility and ensure access to modern energy services. Workforce transition programs and regional development initiatives support communities affected by the decline of fossil fuel industries.

Balancing energy security with climate commitments requires pragmatic planning that aligns short-term reliability with long-term sustainability. Coordinated policy, technological innovation, and international cooperation create the foundation for energy systems that are both resilient and low-carbon.

Chapter 6: Energy Governance, Policy, and Institutional Frameworks

Energy governance, policy, and institutional frameworks determine how societies produce, distribute, and consume energy. These structures shape national strategies, regulatory systems, and investment environments that influence the pace and direction of energy transitions. Effective governance ensures that energy systems are reliable, inclusive, and environmentally sustainable, balancing economic development with social and ecological priorities. Institutions and policies guide decision-making, coordinate across sectors, and create accountability. This chapter explores how transparent governance, coherent policy design, and institutional capacity contribute to achieving energy security and sustainability while fostering resilience in the face of evolving global energy challenges.

Principles of Effective Energy Governance

Effective energy governance provides the institutional and regulatory foundation for achieving energy security, sustainability, and affordability. It encompasses the structures, policies, and decision-making processes that guide how energy is produced, distributed, and consumed. Strong governance ensures that energy systems operate transparently, efficiently, and equitably while supporting economic development and environmental protection.

Clear and coherent policy frameworks are essential for effective energy governance. Governments must establish long-term strategies that align national energy goals with climate commitments and economic priorities. Consistent policies reduce uncertainty for investors and encourage innovation in clean technologies. Integrated energy planning that considers interactions between electricity, transport, and heating sectors helps optimize resource allocation and infrastructure investment. Regulatory stability and transparency strengthen public trust and promote sustained private sector participation.

Institutional coordination is a key principle of energy governance. Energy systems involve multiple actors, including ministries, regulatory agencies, utilities, and private companies. Effective governance requires coordination among these entities to avoid duplication, conflicting mandates, or policy fragmentation. Inter-ministerial committees and independent regulatory bodies enhance coherence between energy, environment, and industrial policies. Decentralized governance structures can improve responsiveness by empowering local authorities to address region-specific challenges while adhering to national objectives.

Transparency and accountability underpin good governance in the energy sector. Decision-making processes must be open, data-driven, and subject to public scrutiny. Publishing energy statistics, regulatory decisions, and policy evaluations ensures that stakeholders can assess progress and hold institutions accountable. Independent oversight bodies and performance audits reinforce institutional integrity and prevent corruption. Public access to information also encourages informed participation and confidence in policy outcomes.

Public participation enhances legitimacy and inclusiveness in energy governance. Engaging citizens, businesses, and civil society in energy planning ensures that diverse perspectives and needs are represented. Participatory mechanisms, such as consultations, hearings, and advisory councils, facilitate collaboration and social acceptance of policy measures. Inclusion of marginalized groups, including women, rural populations, and low-income communities, promotes equitable access to energy services and fair distribution of benefits.

Regulatory effectiveness is another cornerstone of energy governance. Independent regulators must ensure fair competition, cost-reflective tariffs, and non-discriminatory access to networks. Clear rules for licensing, pricing, and interconnection promote market efficiency and investor confidence. Regulators also play a critical role in overseeing quality of service, consumer protection, and environmental compliance. Adopting adaptive regulatory approaches allows systems to respond to technological advancements and evolving market conditions.

Data and evidence-based decision-making improve policy design and implementation. Reliable data on energy supply, demand, prices, and emissions enable informed planning and monitoring. Developing national energy information systems supports forecasting and scenario analysis. Evidence-based policymaking reduces reliance on short-term political considerations and strengthens the link between policy intent and outcomes. Cooperation between statistical agencies, research institutions, and industry enhances data accuracy and availability.

Flexibility and adaptability are vital in managing the evolving energy landscape. Rapid technological change, market shifts, and climate risks require governance frameworks capable of responding to uncertainty. Adaptive policies that incorporate regular review mechanisms ensure continuous improvement and relevance. Scenario planning and risk assessments help anticipate disruptions and prepare for long-term transitions. Resilient governance structures can maintain stability during crises while facilitating innovation and reform.

International cooperation strengthens national governance through the exchange of best practices, harmonization of standards, and shared investment frameworks. Participation in regional energy markets and global initiatives promotes efficiency and energy security. Collaboration on cross-border infrastructure, technology transfer, and capacity building supports equitable progress toward sustainable energy systems. International partnerships also enhance transparency and accountability in global energy governance.

Effective energy governance depends on the balance between central authority and stakeholder participation, long-term planning and adaptability, and market mechanisms and regulatory oversight. When these principles are aligned, governance systems can deliver reliable, sustainable, and inclusive energy outcomes that meet national and global objectives.

National Energy Policies and Long-Term Planning

National energy policies and long-term planning establish the foundation for secure, sustainable, and affordable energy systems. They define strategic priorities, guide investment, and ensure that short-term actions align with long-term objectives such as economic growth, social development, and climate resilience. Effective planning integrates economic, environmental, and technological considerations within a coherent policy framework that responds to evolving national and global conditions.

Comprehensive national energy policies articulate clear goals for energy security, access, and sustainability. They outline pathways for diversification of energy sources, promote efficiency, and encourage innovation. These policies are typically developed through extensive consultation among government agencies, industry stakeholders, and civil society to ensure inclusiveness and transparency. Establishing clear priorities provides stability for investors and directs resources toward strategic areas such as renewable energy expansion, infrastructure modernization, and research and development.

Long-term energy planning requires accurate forecasting of demand and supply. Planners must assess population growth, industrial activity, technological advancement, and urbanization trends to project future energy needs. Scenario analysis helps governments evaluate alternative pathways and their implications for economic and environmental outcomes. Balancing energy demand with sustainable supply involves managing trade-offs between affordability, reliability, and emissions reduction. Planning also accounts for uncertainties such as fluctuating fuel prices, geopolitical risks, and extreme weather events that could disrupt supply chains.

Energy diversification is a key element of national energy strategies. Reducing reliance on a single fuel source enhances resilience against market shocks and supply interruptions. Many countries pursue a mix of fossil fuels, renewables, and emerging technologies such as hydrogen and advanced nuclear energy to achieve balanced energy portfolios. Diversification supports energy independence and allows flexibility in responding to shifts in global energy markets. Integrating domestic resource development with international energy cooperation further strengthens national resilience.

Infrastructure investment forms the backbone of long-term energy planning. Expanding and upgrading electricity grids, pipelines, and storage facilities ensures that energy systems can meet future demand efficiently. Investments in digital infrastructure, such as smart grids and metering systems, improve system flexibility and enable integration of decentralized renewable energy. Modern infrastructure supports innovation and enhances reliability while minimizing technical losses. Governments often employ public–private partnerships and blended finance models to mobilize capital for large-scale projects.

Regulatory frameworks and market structures play a crucial role in implementing national energy policies. Transparent and predictable regulations create an environment conducive to investment and innovation. Policy instruments such as feed-in tariffs, auctions, and tax incentives encourage renewable energy deployment and efficiency improvements. Competitive energy markets can drive innovation and cost reductions, while regulatory oversight ensures consumer protection and equitable access. Adaptive regulation allows governments to respond effectively to new technologies and market developments.

Sustainability and environmental considerations are increasingly central to national energy planning. Integrating climate objectives into energy policy supports national commitments under international agreements. Transitioning to low-carbon energy systems requires aligning emission reduction targets with economic and social priorities. Policies promoting energy efficiency, clean technologies, and carbon capture contribute to reducing the environmental footprint of energy production and consumption. Environmental assessments ensure that new projects align with sustainability principles and minimize ecosystem impacts.

Public participation enhances the legitimacy and effectiveness of national energy policies. Engaging local communities, industry, and academia fosters shared ownership and facilitates smoother implementation. Transparent communication of policy goals and progress builds public confidence and encourages behavioral change toward sustainable energy use. Education and awareness programs strengthen understanding of energy challenges and promote support for long-term reforms.

Monitoring and evaluation mechanisms ensure that national energy policies remain effective and responsive. Regular policy reviews, supported by data collection and performance indicators, allow for adjustments in response to new challenges and opportunities. Institutional capacity building enhances governance and enables continuous improvement in planning and implementation. Long-term energy planning, grounded in robust policy frameworks and inclusive governance, ensures that national energy systems remain resilient, efficient, and aligned with sustainable development goals.

Multi-Level Governance and International Cooperation

Multi-level governance and international cooperation are essential for managing the complex and interconnected nature of global energy systems. Effective coordination among local, national, regional, and international actors ensures that energy policies are coherent, equitable, and aligned with shared sustainability goals. As the energy transition accelerates, collaboration across governance levels becomes increasingly important for addressing climate change, maintaining energy security, and supporting economic development.

At the national level, governments set the overall direction of energy policy through legislation, regulation, and planning frameworks. They define energy security priorities, renewable energy targets, and emission reduction commitments. Coordination across ministries and agencies ensures that policies in sectors such as transport, industry, and environment are consistent and mutually reinforcing. Strong institutions with clear mandates enhance policy implementation and oversight. Decentralization of authority, where appropriate, allows regional and local governments to tailor policies to specific resource conditions and community needs.

Local and regional authorities play a critical role in energy governance. They manage infrastructure planning, land use, and implementation of renewable energy projects. Local governments are also instrumental in promoting energy efficiency, sustainable transport, and decentralized energy systems such as district heating and community solar programs. Their proximity to citizens enables them to engage communities, build public support, and ensure that transition measures reflect local priorities. Effective vertical coordination between local and national authorities aligns resource allocation and policy objectives, improving overall governance performance.

Regional cooperation enhances energy security and market integration. Neighboring countries benefit from shared infrastructure such as electricity interconnections, gas pipelines, and renewable resource zones. Regional energy markets promote competition, increase efficiency, and allow for the balancing of variable renewable generation across borders. Harmonization of regulations and technical standards facilitates trade and investment, while regional institutions help coordinate cross-border planning and dispute resolution. Examples include regional power pools, joint renewable energy auctions, and collaborative research programs that leverage economies of scale.

International cooperation provides the broader framework for achieving global energy and climate goals. Multilateral organizations, such as the International Energy Agency,

International Renewable Energy Agency, and United Nations bodies, support knowledge sharing, capacity building, and policy alignment. Global initiatives help mobilize finance for clean energy deployment and foster technology transfer to developing economies. International agreements on climate change and energy efficiency establish common principles and accountability mechanisms that guide national and regional actions.

Technology and knowledge exchange are key components of international cooperation. Joint research programs, innovation partnerships, and demonstration projects accelerate the development and diffusion of advanced technologies such as energy storage, hydrogen, and carbon capture. Collaborative efforts also promote best practices in regulatory reform, market design, and governance. Access to global data and analytical tools enables countries to make informed decisions about energy investment and policy direction.

Financial cooperation supports countries with limited resources in achieving energy and climate objectives. International financial institutions, development banks, and climate funds provide concessional finance, guarantees, and grants to support energy infrastructure, policy reform, and institutional strengthening. Blended finance mechanisms attract private investment by reducing project risk. Technical assistance programs help governments design regulatory frameworks and build administrative capacity to manage complex energy transitions.

Effective multi-level governance requires transparency, accountability, and stakeholder participation at all levels. Coordinated planning processes, regular communication, and inclusive decision-making ensure that national and local priorities are harmonized with regional and international commitments. Establishing mechanisms for dialogue among public authorities, private sector actors, and civil society fosters trust and facilitates policy coherence.

The combination of multi-level governance and international cooperation enables countries to align domestic energy strategies with global sustainability goals. By integrating efforts across scales, governments can enhance energy system resilience, promote equitable development, and contribute to a stable and secure global energy future.

Transparency, Accountability, and Public Participation

Transparency, accountability, and public participation are fundamental components of effective energy governance. They ensure that decision-making processes are open, inclusive, and based on evidence, which strengthens trust among stakeholders and improves the quality of energy policy outcomes. By integrating these principles into planning, regulation, and implementation, governments can enhance legitimacy, reduce corruption, and align energy development with public interest.

Transparency in energy governance requires access to information at all stages of policy formulation and implementation. Governments and regulatory agencies should provide timely and accurate data on energy production, consumption, prices, and emissions. Publishing policy documents, performance indicators, and project evaluations enables public oversight and informed participation. Transparent procedures for licensing, procurement, and subsidy allocation reduce opportunities for misuse of resources and strengthen investor confidence. Open data platforms and digital portals further facilitate accessibility, enabling researchers, businesses, and citizens to analyze trends and hold institutions accountable.

Accountability ensures that decision-makers and institutions are responsible for their actions and outcomes. Establishing clear roles and mandates for ministries, regulators, and utilities helps avoid overlap and improve coordination. Performance-based management systems link institutional goals to measurable results, allowing for regular monitoring and evaluation. Independent oversight bodies, such as energy regulators, audit agencies, and anti-corruption commissions, provide checks and balances to prevent abuse of authority. Public reporting requirements and parliamentary scrutiny enhance transparency in budget allocation and project execution. Legal frameworks that define penalties for non-compliance reinforce accountability and promote ethical conduct in the energy sector.

Public participation strengthens the legitimacy and inclusiveness of energy policy processes. Involving citizens, industry representatives, academia, and civil society organizations ensures that policies reflect diverse perspectives and needs. Early consultation during policy design helps identify potential social and environmental impacts, reducing conflict and improving implementation outcomes. Participatory approaches, including stakeholder forums, community meetings, and public hearings, provide opportunities for dialogue and collaboration. Engaging marginalized groups and underrepresented communities promotes social equity and ensures that energy access and benefits are distributed fairly.

Technological tools enhance transparency and participation by improving access to information and communication. Online consultation platforms, open-data dashboards, and social media channels allow stakeholders to provide feedback and monitor progress. Geographic information systems (GIS) and mapping tools make energy infrastructure plans and environmental assessments publicly accessible, increasing awareness and oversight. The use of digital tools also enables greater citizen involvement in local energy planning, such as community renewable projects and demand management initiatives.

Capacity building is necessary to support meaningful participation and accountability. Public institutions require training and resources to manage transparent processes effectively, while citizens need awareness and education to engage constructively in policy discussions. Building institutional capacity for data management, performance monitoring, and stakeholder engagement strengthens overall governance. Partnerships with universities, research institutions, and non-governmental organizations can enhance technical expertise and foster innovation in public oversight mechanisms.

International standards and best practices play an important role in promoting transparency and accountability in energy governance. Frameworks such as the Extractive Industries Transparency Initiative (EITI) and the Open Government Partnership encourage governments to disclose key information about resource management and policy decisions. Adoption of these standards enhances credibility in international markets and supports cooperation among governments, investors, and civil society. Global reporting mechanisms and peer reviews facilitate knowledge sharing and continuous improvement in governance practices.

Effective grievance and redress mechanisms further reinforce accountability and public trust. Citizens should have accessible channels to raise concerns about energy projects, regulatory decisions, or service quality. Independent arbitration or mediation processes can resolve disputes fairly and prevent escalation. Ensuring that feedback is incorporated into decision-making promotes continuous improvement and responsiveness in policy implementation.

Institutionalizing transparency, accountability, and participation within energy governance frameworks contributes to fairer and more sustainable outcomes. These principles ensure that energy systems serve the public good, respond to evolving needs, and maintain integrity throughout the transition toward low-carbon and inclusive energy futures.

Chapter 7: Financing Energy Security and Sustainable Transitions

Financing energy security and sustainable transitions is essential for achieving reliable, inclusive, and low-carbon energy systems. The scale of investment required to expand access, modernize infrastructure, and decarbonize supply is unprecedented, demanding coordinated action from public and private sectors. Sustainable finance directs capital toward projects that enhance energy resilience while supporting environmental and social goals. Policy frameworks, green financial instruments, and innovative funding models play a critical role in mobilizing resources. This chapter explores the mechanisms, partnerships, and policy tools needed to ensure that financial flows align with global commitments to energy security and sustainable development.

Global Investment Needs for Sustainable Energy

Achieving a sustainable global energy system requires significant and sustained investment across all sectors of the economy. Transitioning from fossil fuel dependency to a low-carbon energy system entails large-scale deployment of renewable energy, modernization of infrastructure, improvement of energy efficiency, and expansion of access to modern energy services. These investment needs are influenced by population growth, economic development, technological advancement, and policy ambition.

Investment in renewable energy generation forms the cornerstone of sustainable energy financing. Expanding solar, wind, hydropower, and geothermal capacity requires substantial upfront capital but delivers long-term environmental and economic benefits. Utility-scale renewable projects attract large institutional investors, while decentralized systems such as rooftop solar and mini-grids rely more heavily on private and community investment. Ensuring a stable policy environment with predictable tariffs, clear regulations, and grid access incentives helps attract financing from domestic and international sources.

Modernizing electricity grids and expanding transmission infrastructure are critical to integrating variable renewable energy into national and regional power systems. Upgrading grids improves efficiency, reduces losses, and enhances reliability. Investment is needed for advanced metering, digital monitoring systems, and energy storage to balance fluctuating supply and demand. Cross-border interconnections support regional power trade, optimizing the use of renewable resources and reducing overall generation costs. Public–private partnerships can play an important role in financing large-scale transmission projects that have long payback periods but substantial social benefits.

Energy efficiency investments offer one of the most cost-effective means of reducing energy demand and emissions. Efficiency improvements across industry, buildings, and transport sectors reduce the overall scale of required energy infrastructure while lowering operating costs for consumers and businesses. Financial instruments such as green bonds, performance-based incentives, and low-interest loans encourage investment in energy-efficient technologies. Policy frameworks that set minimum efficiency standards for appliances, vehicles, and industrial equipment further accelerate progress.

Expanding energy access in developing countries requires targeted investments in infrastructure, technology, and capacity building. More than 700 million people worldwide still lack access to electricity, and billions rely on traditional biomass for cooking. Investment in decentralized renewable systems, including solar mini-grids and clean cooking technologies, is essential to achieve universal energy access. Blended finance models that combine concessional funding with private capital help overcome high upfront costs and perceived investment risks in underserved markets. Ensuring affordability for end users remains a key challenge that requires careful policy design and social protection mechanisms.

Investment in research, development, and innovation drives technological progress and cost reductions. Emerging technologies such as green hydrogen, advanced batteries, carbon capture, and next-generation nuclear power require sustained public and private funding. Public research institutions, private companies, and multilateral agencies must collaborate to accelerate commercialization and deployment. Innovation clusters and technology partnerships create environments where knowledge sharing and experimentation flourish, promoting faster diffusion of sustainable technologies.

Mobilizing finance at the scale required for the global energy transition demands a mix of public and private funding sources. Governments provide foundational support through policy frameworks, subsidies, and risk mitigation instruments, while private investors contribute capital and operational expertise. Institutional investors such as pension funds and sovereign wealth funds are increasingly incorporating sustainability criteria into their portfolios. International financial institutions and climate funds play a vital role in channeling resources to developing economies, where investment gaps remain largest.

Policy stability and clear market signals are critical to attracting long-term investment. Carbon pricing, fossil fuel subsidy reform, and transparent regulatory systems guide capital toward low-carbon projects. Governments can strengthen investor confidence by establishing consistent policies, reducing administrative barriers, and ensuring transparent procurement processes. Financial de-risking instruments, such as guarantees and insurance mechanisms, help attract private capital to markets with higher perceived risks.

Equity considerations must also be integrated into global investment strategies. The transition to sustainable energy should promote inclusive growth and ensure that benefits are distributed fairly across societies. Investments in education, training, and social infrastructure can help create new employment opportunities and reduce disparities. International cooperation can facilitate equitable access to finance, technology, and capacity development.

Global investment needs for sustainable energy are substantial but achievable with coordinated international effort and policy coherence. Strategic public investment, supportive regulation, and mobilization of private finance together can deliver the infrastructure and innovation necessary to meet the dual goals of universal energy access and climate stability.

Innovative Financial Mechanisms and Green Bonds

Innovative financial mechanisms are reshaping how sustainable energy projects are financed, enabling greater private sector participation and reducing risks associated with large-scale energy investments. As the world moves toward low-carbon development, the demand for creative financing tools has grown to bridge funding gaps and accelerate the transition to clean energy systems. Among these mechanisms, green bonds have emerged as a prominent instrument for mobilizing capital toward environmentally sustainable projects.

Green bonds are debt securities issued to finance projects that deliver environmental benefits, including renewable energy, energy efficiency, and climate adaptation initiatives. Their structure is similar to traditional bonds, but proceeds are earmarked for sustainable activities. Investors benefit from stable returns while contributing to environmental objectives. Transparency and accountability are maintained through certification and reporting frameworks that verify the environmental integrity of funded projects. The rapid growth of the green bond market reflects increasing investor demand for assets aligned with sustainability criteria and global commitments to net-zero targets.

Sovereign, municipal, and corporate issuers are increasingly turning to green bonds to fund sustainable energy infrastructure. Governments use green bonds to finance national renewable energy programs, grid expansion, and energy-efficient public buildings. Corporations issue them to invest in clean production technologies and sustainable supply chains. Financial institutions and development banks also play a key role by providing guarantees, underwriting services, and technical assistance to improve market confidence. Standardized taxonomies and guidelines, such as those from the International Capital Market Association, enhance transparency and comparability across issuances.

Blended finance mechanisms combine public and private funding to reduce risks for investors and attract capital to markets where financing remains limited. By using public funds to absorb early-stage or political risks, blended finance structures encourage private investors to engage in projects they might otherwise avoid. Instruments such as concessional loans, first-loss guarantees, and risk-sharing facilities can be particularly effective in supporting clean energy investments in developing economies. Partnerships between development finance institutions, commercial banks, and governments enable more equitable access to funding while maintaining financial viability.

Results-based financing links disbursement of funds to measurable outcomes, ensuring accountability and efficiency. In the energy sector, this approach can incentivize renewable generation, energy efficiency improvements, or emissions reductions by rewarding verified performance. Results-based mechanisms align financial incentives with sustainability goals and encourage innovation by tying funding to tangible impact rather than upfront costs. Such models are increasingly used in energy access programs, where outcomes such as electrification rates or energy savings determine payments to project developers.

Carbon pricing and market-based instruments provide additional financial incentives for clean energy investment. Emissions trading systems and carbon taxes internalize the environmental costs of fossil fuel use, making renewable energy more competitive. Revenues generated from carbon pricing can be reinvested in green infrastructure, research, and social protection measures to ensure a fair transition. These instruments create predictable price signals that guide investors toward low-carbon technologies and improve the overall efficiency of energy markets.

Energy service companies (ESCOs) and performance contracting offer another innovative financing model. Under this arrangement, ESCOs implement energy efficiency projects and are repaid from the cost savings achieved. This eliminates the need for large upfront investment from clients and promotes long-term efficiency gains. The model is widely used in public buildings, industrial facilities, and commercial sectors where operational cost savings can be quantified and verified.

Digital finance and fintech innovations are expanding access to clean energy investment opportunities. Crowdfunding platforms, peer-to-peer lending, and tokenized assets allow smaller investors to participate in renewable energy projects. Digital tools also improve transparency by enabling real-time tracking of investments and performance metrics. These mechanisms democratize energy finance, increase public engagement, and diversify funding sources for sustainable energy systems.

International financial cooperation supports the development and scaling of innovative mechanisms. Multilateral development banks and climate funds provide technical assistance and concessional financing to establish local green bond markets and blended finance platforms. Collaborative initiatives promote knowledge exchange, harmonize standards, and enhance the credibility of sustainable finance instruments. The expansion of these innovative mechanisms ensures that financial flows align with the goals of a sustainable, inclusive, and resilient global energy transition.

Role of Development Banks and Climate Finance

Development banks and climate finance play a critical role in accelerating the transition to sustainable energy systems, particularly in developing economies where investment gaps remain significant. By providing long-term capital, risk mitigation instruments, and technical expertise, these institutions bridge the divide between public policy goals and private sector participation. Their actions mobilize financing for renewable energy, energy efficiency, and adaptation projects that contribute to achieving global climate and development objectives.

Multilateral development banks (MDBs) such as the World Bank, the Asian Development Bank, and the African Development Bank are central to financing sustainable energy infrastructure. They offer concessional loans, grants, and guarantees that reduce the financial risks associated with large-scale renewable projects. MDBs also support policy reforms and capacity building to strengthen the institutional environment for clean energy investment. Through technical assistance and advisory services, they help governments design regulatory frameworks that attract private capital and promote sustainable energy markets.

National development banks complement these efforts by channeling domestic resources toward green investments. They operate at the intersection of public policy and private finance, aligning their portfolios with national climate strategies. By providing credit lines to local banks and investors, national development banks increase the availability of affordable financing for renewable energy and energy efficiency projects. Their understanding of local markets allows them to identify bankable projects and support innovation, particularly among small and medium-sized enterprises engaged in clean energy development.

Climate finance mechanisms are designed to support mitigation and adaptation actions in line with international commitments under the Paris Agreement. The Green Climate Fund (GCF), the Global Environment Facility (GEF), and the Climate Investment Funds (CIF) are among the largest dedicated sources of climate-related funding. These mechanisms provide grants, concessional loans, and guarantees that lower financing barriers in developing countries. By co-financing projects with development banks and private investors, they leverage additional capital for sustainable energy deployment and strengthen resilience to climate impacts.

Blended finance is an increasingly important approach in climate finance, combining concessional public funding with commercial investment to achieve development and climate outcomes. By using public funds to de-risk private investment, blended finance mechanisms make renewable energy projects more attractive to institutional investors. Instruments such as first-loss capital, subordinated debt, and political risk insurance are widely used to mitigate risks associated with currency fluctuations, policy uncertainty, and project performance. This approach has proven effective in mobilizing large-scale investment for renewable energy and energy access initiatives.

Development banks also play a catalytic role in mobilizing private sector financing through partnerships and co-investment platforms. By providing anchor investments and guarantees, they reduce perceived risks and crowd in private capital. Public–private partnerships supported by development finance institutions enable the construction of large renewable energy plants, grid infrastructure, and sustainable transport systems. Development banks' participation provides credibility and confidence to investors, ensuring that projects meet international standards of governance, environmental protection, and social inclusion.

Technical assistance provided by development banks and climate funds enhances institutional capacity and project readiness. Governments benefit from support in project preparation, feasibility studies, and financial structuring. Capacity building programs help regulators, utilities, and financial institutions strengthen governance frameworks and integrate sustainability criteria into investment decisions. Technical support also promotes the adoption of international best practices in procurement, monitoring, and evaluation, ensuring transparency and accountability in project implementation.

Climate finance tracking and reporting are essential for maintaining transparency and ensuring that funds are directed toward genuine climate objectives. Development banks have developed frameworks to assess the climate relevance of their portfolios and monitor the impact of financed projects. Harmonized methodologies for measuring emissions reductions and resilience benefits improve comparability and accountability across institutions. Transparent reporting enhances trust among stakeholders and demonstrates progress toward national and global climate goals.

Development banks and climate finance institutions are instrumental in shaping the global transition to sustainable energy. Their capacity to mobilize large-scale investment, foster innovation, and build institutional resilience allows countries to pursue low-carbon development pathways while maintaining economic growth and social inclusion.

Private Sector Engagement and Risk Mitigation

Private sector engagement is essential for scaling up investment in sustainable energy systems. The transition to low-carbon energy requires capital and innovation that exceed the capacity of public funding alone. Private companies, investors, and financial institutions contribute through technology development, infrastructure financing, and operational expertise. Effective risk mitigation mechanisms and policy frameworks are necessary to attract private participation and ensure that investments align with long-term sustainability goals.

The private sector plays a central role in developing, constructing, and operating renewable energy projects. Independent power producers, utilities, and developers invest in solar, wind, hydro, and biomass projects that expand clean energy generation capacity. Equipment manufacturers and technology firms drive innovation in energy efficiency, storage, and grid management. Financial institutions, including commercial banks, private equity funds, and institutional investors, provide capital for large-scale infrastructure and distributed energy systems. The diversity of private sector actors strengthens competition, reduces costs, and accelerates the deployment of sustainable technologies.

Policy and regulatory certainty are key to encouraging private investment. Investors require stable and transparent frameworks that define market rules, tariffs, and grid access conditions. Clear long-term policy signals, such as renewable energy targets and carbon pricing, improve predictability and reduce perceived risks. Governments can enhance investor confidence by ensuring consistent enforcement of contracts, timely permitting, and predictable subsidy structures. Removing fossil fuel subsidies and streamlining regulatory processes further level the playing field for clean energy investment.

Public–private partnerships (PPPs) are a key mechanism for leveraging private capital in sustainable energy infrastructure. In PPP models, the public sector provides policy direction and often shares financial risks through guarantees, co-financing, or long-term offtake agreements. Private partners contribute technical expertise, efficiency in project delivery, and operational management. These partnerships enable large-scale investments in renewable generation, transmission networks, and energy efficiency retrofits that might otherwise be difficult to finance. Successful PPPs require well-defined contractual frameworks, transparent procurement processes, and balanced risk allocation between public and private entities.

Risk mitigation instruments are essential to mobilize private investment in emerging and developing markets, where perceived or actual risks can deter participation. Political risk insurance, provided by organizations such as the Multilateral Investment Guarantee Agency, protects investors from risks related to expropriation, currency inconvertibility, or contract breaches. Credit enhancement tools, such as partial risk and partial credit guarantees, improve the creditworthiness of projects and reduce financing costs. Currency hedging facilities help manage exchange rate volatility, while liquidity support mechanisms ensure project stability in the event of market disruptions.

Blended finance approaches combine public and private resources to address risk barriers and make sustainable energy projects more bankable. Concessional funding from development finance institutions can absorb higher-risk portions of investment structures, encouraging private investors to participate. First-loss capital, subordinated debt, and co-investment platforms are effective instruments for attracting institutional investors to renewable energy portfolios. Blended finance not only reduces risk but also demonstrates the commercial viability of sustainable projects, paving the way for further market-based investment.

Innovative contractual arrangements such as power purchase agreements (PPAs) and feed-in tariffs provide revenue certainty for investors and lenders. Long-term PPAs between renewable energy producers and utilities or large consumers guarantee stable income streams, improving project bankability. Corporate PPAs, where companies procure renewable electricity directly from generators, are increasingly used to meet sustainability targets and hedge against future energy price volatility. These instruments align corporate climate commitments with national renewable energy objectives.

Access to reliable data and performance standards further reduces investment risk. Transparent information on project pipelines, resource assessments, and regulatory compliance helps investors make informed decisions. International certification schemes and due diligence frameworks ensure that projects meet environmental, social, and governance criteria. Adoption of standardized contracts and reporting practices simplifies project evaluation and promotes investor confidence.

Engaging the private sector in sustainable energy development requires a supportive ecosystem of financial instruments, regulatory stability, and transparent governance. By mitigating risks and aligning incentives, governments and financial institutions can harness private capital and expertise to accelerate the global transition toward resilient and sustainable energy systems.

Chapter 8: Technological Innovation and the Future of Energy Systems

Technological innovation is transforming how energy is produced, distributed, and consumed, shaping the future of global energy systems. Advances in renewable technologies, digitalization, storage solutions, and smart grids are enhancing efficiency, flexibility, and resilience. These innovations support the transition toward low-carbon economies while expanding access to clean and affordable energy. The convergence of artificial intelligence, data analytics, and automation is also redefining system management and decision-making. This chapter examines the role of technology in driving sustainable energy transitions, exploring how innovation can accelerate progress toward secure, inclusive, and environmentally responsible energy futures.

Emerging Technologies in Energy Generation and Storage

Emerging technologies in energy generation and storage are redefining how energy is produced, managed, and consumed. Advances in renewable energy, advanced materials, digital systems, and electrochemical storage are driving efficiency, resilience, and sustainability. These innovations are essential for achieving global decarbonization targets, enhancing energy access, and supporting the transition toward more flexible and integrated energy systems.

Solar power continues to lead innovation in renewable energy. Photovoltaic (PV) technologies have evolved beyond traditional silicon-based systems to include perovskite, thin-film, and tandem solar cells that achieve higher conversion efficiencies and lower production costs. Floating solar installations expand the potential for solar deployment on reservoirs and coastal areas, while building-integrated photovoltaics integrate solar generation directly into infrastructure. Advances in manufacturing and recycling processes are improving sustainability across the solar value chain, reducing material use and energy intensity in production.

Wind energy technology has advanced through larger turbine designs, improved blade aerodynamics, and offshore development. Modern turbines operate efficiently at varying wind speeds and can generate electricity in low-wind regions once considered unsuitable. Offshore wind is expanding rapidly due to its higher capacity factors and the availability of larger project areas. Floating offshore wind platforms extend deployment into deep waters, enabling new markets with significant wind potential. Integration with digital monitoring systems and predictive maintenance tools enhances operational performance and reduces costs.

Hydrogen is emerging as a versatile energy carrier with applications in power generation, transport, and industrial processes. Green hydrogen, produced through water electrolysis powered by renewable energy, offers a zero-emission alternative to fossil-based hydrogen. Advances in electrolyzer technologies, including proton exchange membrane and solid oxide systems, are improving efficiency and scalability. Hydrogen storage and transport remain challenges, but ongoing research into liquefaction, compression, and carrier materials is expanding its potential. Hydrogen can also be used in fuel cells for electricity generation or combined with carbon dioxide to produce synthetic fuels.

Bioenergy technologies are evolving toward more sustainable feedstocks and advanced conversion processes. Second-generation biofuels utilize agricultural residues and non-food biomass, reducing pressure on food supply chains. Biogas from anaerobic digestion and biochar from pyrolysis provide additional renewable energy sources while improving soil health and waste management. Integration of bioenergy with carbon capture and storage (BECCS) has the potential to deliver negative emissions, making it a strategic component in achieving net-zero targets.

Geothermal energy continues to expand through enhanced geothermal systems that extract heat from deeper, less permeable rock formations. Advances in drilling techniques and reservoir stimulation have increased the geographic reach of geothermal resources. Geothermal plants provide reliable baseload power with low emissions, making them valuable for energy systems seeking both stability and sustainability. The use of geothermal heat pumps in buildings also improves energy efficiency by providing heating and cooling with minimal environmental impact.

Energy storage technologies are advancing rapidly to address the variability of renewable energy generation. Lithium-ion batteries dominate the market due to their high energy density and declining costs, but alternative chemistries such as sodium-ion, solid-state, and flow batteries are emerging to address limitations in scalability, safety, and resource availability. Flow batteries, which store energy in liquid electrolytes, are particularly suited for large-scale, long-duration storage applications. Thermal and mechanical storage systems, including molten salt, compressed air, and gravity-based storage, complement electrochemical solutions by offering different discharge durations and operational profiles.

Integration of digital technologies enhances the performance and coordination of emerging energy systems. Artificial intelligence, machine learning, and the Internet of Things optimize generation, storage, and consumption through real-time data analysis. Predictive maintenance reduces downtime and extends asset lifespans, while advanced forecasting improves grid stability by anticipating fluctuations in renewable generation. Blockchain-based systems enable peer-to-peer energy trading and transparent verification of renewable energy credits, fostering decentralized and democratized energy markets.

Advanced nuclear technologies, including small modular reactors and next-generation fission designs, are being developed to provide flexible, low-carbon baseload power. These systems aim to improve safety, reduce waste, and enhance cost-effectiveness through modular construction and passive safety features. Research into nuclear fusion continues to progress, offering the potential for nearly limitless, clean energy if technological and economic challenges can be overcome.

Emerging technologies in energy generation and storage are expanding the range of options available for achieving reliable, low-carbon energy systems. Continued investment in research, innovation, and infrastructure will determine the speed and scale at which these technologies reshape global energy landscapes.

Hydrogen, Carbon Capture, and Negative Emissions

Hydrogen, carbon capture, and negative emissions technologies are becoming central components of strategies to achieve deep decarbonization across energy systems. Each plays a distinct but complementary role in reducing greenhouse gas emissions and enabling a transition to net-zero economies. Together, they support the decarbonization of hard-to-abate sectors such as heavy industry, long-distance transport, and power generation while contributing to broader climate stabilization goals.

Hydrogen is a versatile energy carrier that can replace fossil fuels in sectors where direct electrification is challenging. It can be used for power generation, heating, industrial processes, and transport. The environmental impact of hydrogen depends on its production method. Green hydrogen, produced through electrolysis using renewable electricity, generates no carbon emissions. Blue hydrogen, derived from natural gas with carbon capture and storage (CCS), offers a lower-emission alternative during the transition to fully renewable systems. Ongoing research and investment aim to reduce the cost of electrolyzers, improve efficiency, and expand hydrogen infrastructure for production, storage, and distribution.

Hydrogen storage and transport are key challenges in scaling its use. Its low energy density requires high-pressure tanks, liquefaction, or conversion into carrier compounds such as ammonia or methanol. Advances in materials science are enabling safer and more efficient storage solutions, while international cooperation is developing standards and networks for global hydrogen trade. Hydrogen can also serve as a seasonal storage medium for balancing renewable energy generation, allowing surplus power from solar and wind to be converted and stored for later use.

Carbon capture, utilization, and storage technologies are essential for managing emissions from existing fossil fuel infrastructure and industrial processes. CCS involves capturing carbon dioxide (CO_2) from power plants or industrial sources, transporting it via pipelines, and storing it in geological formations such as depleted oil fields or saline aquifers. Utilization pathways, including the conversion of captured CO_2 into fuels, building materials, or chemicals, offer potential economic benefits while reducing net emissions. Large-scale deployment of CCS requires substantial investment in infrastructure, monitoring, and regulation to ensure environmental safety and long-term storage integrity.

Carbon capture technology is also being integrated into natural gas processing, cement production, and steelmaking, sectors where process emissions are difficult to eliminate. Post-combustion and pre-combustion capture systems, along with emerging technologies such as direct air capture (DAC), are being refined to improve efficiency and reduce costs. DAC systems remove CO_2 directly from the atmosphere, offering a means of addressing historical emissions and achieving negative emission outcomes. While current costs remain high, scaling production and increasing renewable energy use in DAC operations can enhance feasibility.

Negative emissions technologies (NETs) encompass a range of approaches that remove CO_2 from the atmosphere to offset residual emissions. In addition to DAC, these include bioenergy with carbon capture and storage (BECCS), afforestation and reforestation, soil carbon sequestration, and ocean-based carbon removal. BECCS combines biomass energy production with CCS, capturing carbon released during combustion and storing it permanently underground. This process can generate electricity while achieving net-negative emissions, though its scalability depends on sustainable biomass supply and careful land-use management.

Nature-based solutions remain critical components of the negative emissions portfolio. Forest restoration, wetland rehabilitation, and regenerative agriculture enhance carbon storage in ecosystems while delivering co-benefits such as biodiversity protection and water regulation. These measures complement technological approaches and can be implemented immediately using existing knowledge and infrastructure. However, they require robust governance to ensure permanence, prevent land-use conflicts, and maintain ecological balance.

Financial and policy support are vital for accelerating the deployment of hydrogen, CCS, and NETs. Governments can stimulate investment through tax incentives, contracts for difference, and public–private partnerships. International cooperation and harmonized standards facilitate technology transfer and global market development. Transparent carbon accounting frameworks are needed to ensure that captured or removed carbon is accurately measured and verifiable. Coordinated efforts across research, finance, and policy domains can help integrate these technologies into comprehensive strategies for achieving long-term climate neutrality.

Digitalization, AI, and Smart Energy Management

Digitalization, artificial intelligence (AI), and smart energy management are transforming the operation and governance of modern energy systems. The integration of digital technologies enables real-time monitoring, predictive analysis, and optimized control of energy generation, distribution, and consumption. These advancements enhance efficiency, reliability, and sustainability while supporting the transition to decentralized and low-carbon energy systems.

Digitalization provides the foundation for data-driven energy management. Sensors, meters, and communication networks collect vast amounts of information on system performance, energy flows, and user behavior. This data allows utilities and operators to detect inefficiencies, predict demand fluctuations, and identify maintenance needs before failures occur. Digital platforms enable integrated management of distributed energy resources such as rooftop solar panels, electric vehicles, and battery storage, improving coordination across the grid.

AI plays a crucial role in analyzing complex datasets and automating decision-making processes in energy systems. Machine learning algorithms can forecast electricity demand and renewable generation with high accuracy, allowing operators to balance supply and demand more effectively. AI-driven predictive maintenance identifies potential equipment failures, reducing downtime and operational costs. Optimization algorithms also improve the dispatch of energy resources, ensuring that generation assets operate efficiently while minimizing emissions and costs.

Smart grids exemplify the application of digitalization and AI in electricity networks. Unlike traditional grids that rely on one-way energy flows, smart grids facilitate two-way communication between producers and consumers. They integrate advanced metering infrastructure, automation, and control technologies to manage electricity distribution dynamically. Smart grids enhance resilience by automatically isolating faults, rerouting power, and restoring service after disruptions. They also enable greater penetration of renewable energy by balancing intermittent generation with flexible demand and storage solutions.

Digitalization empowers consumers to participate actively in energy markets. Smart meters provide real-time feedback on energy use, enabling households and businesses to adjust consumption based on price signals or environmental preferences. Demand response programs, supported by digital communication systems, allow consumers to reduce or shift electricity use during peak periods, improving grid stability. Peer-to-peer trading platforms, often based on blockchain technology, enable consumers to buy and sell renewable energy directly within local networks, fostering decentralized energy economies.

In industrial and commercial sectors, AI and digital energy management systems optimize energy use by integrating data from production processes, heating and cooling systems, and building management. Automated controls adjust lighting, temperature, and machinery operation based on occupancy or production schedules. These systems contribute to cost savings, improved productivity, and reduced emissions. Digital twins—virtual models of physical assets—allow operators to simulate performance, test scenarios, and plan maintenance with greater accuracy and efficiency.

Cybersecurity is a growing priority as energy systems become increasingly interconnected and digitalized. Protecting critical infrastructure from cyberattacks requires robust security protocols, encryption technologies, and continuous monitoring. Governments and utilities are adopting standards and frameworks to safeguard data privacy and system integrity. Investments in cybersecurity research and workforce training are essential to maintaining resilience in digital energy systems.

The use of AI in energy markets extends to long-term planning and investment decision-making. Algorithms analyze trends in demand, fuel prices, and technology costs to support policy design and infrastructure development. In renewable energy forecasting, AI models integrate weather data, satellite imagery, and grid conditions to optimize energy dispatch and storage utilization. This reduces uncertainty for investors and improves the financial viability of clean energy projects.

Digitalization and smart technologies also facilitate energy access in developing regions. Remote monitoring, mobile payment systems, and automated maintenance support the operation of off-grid and mini-grid renewable systems. These tools enhance the reliability and affordability of energy services, promoting social and economic development in areas where traditional grid expansion remains difficult.

The convergence of digitalization, AI, and smart energy management is reshaping global energy systems into more intelligent, flexible, and responsive networks. These technologies enable better integration of renewables, improved efficiency, and more equitable participation in energy markets, driving progress toward sustainable and resilient energy futures.

The Role of Innovation Ecosystems and Research Collaboration

Innovation ecosystems and research collaboration are fundamental to advancing sustainable energy technologies and accelerating the global transition to low-carbon economies. By connecting governments, research institutions, private companies, and investors, these systems foster the development, testing, and scaling of solutions that enhance energy security, efficiency, and environmental performance. Effective collaboration promotes knowledge sharing, reduces duplication of effort, and strengthens the ability of nations to address complex energy challenges collectively.

Innovation ecosystems thrive on the interaction between multiple actors working across different stages of technological development. Governments provide strategic direction and funding through policies that support research, demonstration, and deployment. Universities and research institutions contribute foundational knowledge and technical expertise. Private companies bring innovation to market through applied research and commercialization. Financial institutions and venture capital investors play a crucial role by supplying risk capital to emerging technologies with high potential but uncertain returns. The interdependence among these actors creates an environment where ideas can evolve rapidly from concept to implementation.

Public research programs remain essential to early-stage innovation, particularly in areas where commercial incentives are limited. Government-funded laboratories and national research agencies conduct basic and applied research on renewable energy, energy storage, carbon management, and digital technologies. Public support reduces risks for private investment in unproven technologies and ensures that the benefits of innovation are widely distributed. Strategic public investment in research infrastructure, such as testing facilities and pilot plants, provides a foundation for technological advancement and industrial competitiveness.

Collaboration between academia and industry enhances the practical application of research outcomes. Joint projects, innovation hubs, and technology clusters allow for direct exchange between researchers and businesses. Universities contribute advanced technical knowledge and analytical tools, while companies provide operational experience and insights into market demand. These partnerships bridge the gap between discovery and deployment, improving the scalability and cost-effectiveness of new technologies. Cooperative research centers, often supported by public grants, serve as catalysts for collaboration across disciplines and sectors.

International collaboration expands the reach and impact of innovation ecosystems. Cross-border research partnerships facilitate knowledge exchange, technology transfer, and joint development of energy solutions suited to diverse regional contexts. Multilateral frameworks such as Mission Innovation, the International Energy Agency's Technology Collaboration Programs, and regional research networks support joint investments in clean energy research and development. Collaborative initiatives also help harmonize technical standards and regulatory frameworks, improving market integration and global adoption of new technologies.

Innovation ecosystems increasingly rely on open innovation models that encourage the sharing of data, tools, and intellectual property. Open research platforms and digital repositories allow researchers and businesses to access information, reducing duplication and accelerating discovery. Collaborative software and simulation tools enable virtual experimentation and optimization of new energy technologies. Intellectual property sharing through licensing or patent pools fosters wider technology diffusion while maintaining fair incentives for innovators.

Financial mechanisms are integral to sustaining research collaboration. Blended finance, green venture capital, and public–private co-funding schemes provide resources for projects that combine technological innovation with commercial scalability. Development banks and climate funds often support collaborative initiatives that align with national or regional energy priorities. These financing structures reduce risk, attract private investment, and enable early-stage innovations to advance toward commercialization.

Innovation ecosystems benefit from diversity in expertise and participation. Inclusion of small and medium-sized enterprises, local innovators, and community-based organizations broadens the range of ideas and ensures that solutions address social as well as technical challenges. Collaborative programs that involve multiple stakeholders can also enhance public acceptance of new technologies by increasing transparency and demonstrating tangible local benefits.

Capacity building supports the long-term success of innovation ecosystems and collaborative research. Training programs, academic exchanges, and professional development initiatives build the human capital needed to sustain technological progress. Governments and international organizations play an important role in facilitating access to education and research opportunities in developing economies. Strengthening institutional capacity ensures that all countries can contribute to and benefit from global energy innovation.

The success of innovation ecosystems and research collaboration depends on sustained investment, transparent governance, and commitment to shared goals. By aligning research, finance, and policy efforts, these systems drive continuous improvement in energy technologies and create pathways toward more sustainable and resilient energy futures.

Chapter 9: Resilience, Risk Management, and Global Energy Transitions

Resilience and risk management are fundamental to ensuring stable and secure global energy transitions. As energy systems evolve toward low-carbon pathways, they face increasing exposure to physical, economic, and geopolitical risks. Climate change, market volatility, and technological disruptions challenge the reliability and sustainability of supply. Building resilience involves anticipating shocks, diversifying energy sources, and strengthening adaptive capacity across all sectors. Effective risk management supports long-term planning, investment stability, and policy coherence. This chapter explores the frameworks and strategies needed to enhance resilience and manage risks in the ongoing transformation of global energy systems.

Climate Change and Energy System Vulnerabilities

Climate change poses significant risks to the reliability, affordability, and sustainability of global energy systems. Rising temperatures, extreme weather events, and shifting hydrological patterns disrupt energy production, transmission, and consumption. As energy systems form the backbone of economic activity, their vulnerability to climate impacts creates cascading effects across sectors. Addressing these risks requires understanding the physical and systemic vulnerabilities that affect different energy sources and infrastructures.

Thermal power generation, which relies on water for cooling, is increasingly affected by rising temperatures and changing precipitation patterns. Higher ambient temperatures reduce cooling efficiency and limit plant output, while droughts can constrain water availability for operations. In regions where water scarcity is intensifying, competition between energy generation and other water users heightens stress on both resources. Power plants located near coastlines face additional risks from sea-level rise and saltwater intrusion, which can damage equipment and degrade water quality used in cooling processes.

Hydropower systems are highly sensitive to variations in rainfall and snowmelt. Climate-induced shifts in precipitation patterns alter river flows, affecting generation capacity and reliability. Reduced snowpack in mountainous regions diminishes seasonal water storage, leading to lower hydropower output during dry periods. Conversely, increased flooding can damage dams and turbines, disrupt operations, and endanger downstream communities. These impacts underscore the need for adaptive water management and diversified energy portfolios in regions dependent on hydropower.

Renewable energy sources such as wind and solar are also exposed to climate variability. Changes in wind patterns can influence the performance of wind farms, altering expected output and project economics. Prolonged heatwaves may reduce the efficiency of solar photovoltaic systems, while dust storms and air pollution can limit sunlight exposure. Although renewables are generally more resilient than fossil-based systems, they still require adaptive design and location planning to maintain stable generation in a changing climate.

Energy transmission and distribution networks are vulnerable to extreme weather events such as storms, wildfires, and floods. High winds can damage transmission lines and towers, while flooding threatens substations and underground cables. Heatwaves increase the risk of equipment overheating and grid instability, leading to blackouts during periods of peak demand. In wildfire-prone regions, power lines have been linked to ignition events, prompting utilities to adopt preventative shutdowns that disrupt supply. Strengthening grid infrastructure and enhancing operational flexibility are critical measures for managing these physical risks.

The energy demand profile is also changing as a result of climate trends. Rising global temperatures increase the need for air conditioning, particularly in urban and industrialized areas, leading to higher peak electricity demand. At the same time, milder winters may reduce heating requirements in some regions but increase reliance on electric heating in others. These shifts in consumption patterns strain electricity systems, particularly in areas with limited generation or transmission capacity. Energy planners must account for these evolving dynamics when designing future systems and forecasting demand.

Oil and gas production infrastructure faces multiple climate-related challenges. Offshore platforms are exposed to stronger storms and sea-level rise, which can damage facilities and interrupt production. Onshore operations, including pipelines and refineries, are threatened by floods, permafrost thaw, and heat-related equipment degradation. Extreme weather events can also disrupt supply chains and logistics, causing delays in fuel transport and refining. The growing frequency of climate-related disruptions increases financial risks for companies and investors in the fossil fuel sector.

Energy storage systems and critical materials supply chains are emerging areas of vulnerability. Extreme weather can affect battery storage facilities, leading to degradation or failure. The production and transportation of materials essential for renewable technologies—such as lithium, cobalt, and rare earth elements—are concentrated in regions that may experience geopolitical or climate-related instability. Disruptions in these supply chains could slow the global transition to clean energy and increase costs for consumers and manufacturers.

Adaptation measures are increasingly being integrated into energy system planning. Infrastructure design standards are being revised to withstand higher temperatures, stronger winds, and increased precipitation. Relocation of critical facilities away from high-risk zones, such as floodplains and coastlines, reduces exposure to hazards. Enhancing regional interconnections and diversifying generation sources improves resilience by allowing energy systems to absorb and recover from localized disruptions. Investment in advanced forecasting, digital monitoring, and early warning systems enables operators to anticipate and respond to climate threats more effectively.

Policy frameworks play an essential role in addressing energy system vulnerabilities to climate change. National adaptation plans and energy strategies are beginning to include risk assessments, resilience indicators, and financing mechanisms for climate-proofing infrastructure. Coordinated governance between energy, environment, and disaster management institutions improves preparedness and response capacity. Collaboration among governments, utilities, and research institutions supports innovation in resilient technologies and strengthens adaptive capacity across all components of the energy system.

Climate change amplifies existing vulnerabilities in global energy systems through complex and interrelated risks. Understanding and addressing these vulnerabilities is crucial to ensuring that future energy systems remain secure, reliable, and capable of supporting sustainable development under changing climatic conditions.

Energy Resilience and Adaptation Strategies

Energy resilience and adaptation strategies focus on ensuring that energy systems can anticipate, withstand, and recover from climate-related and other external disruptions. As the global energy landscape becomes more interconnected and exposed to environmental and geopolitical risks, building resilience has become a central goal of sustainable energy planning. These strategies involve strengthening physical infrastructure, diversifying energy sources, enhancing system flexibility, and improving institutional coordination to reduce vulnerability and ensure long-term reliability.

Infrastructure resilience is fundamental to maintaining secure energy supply under changing climatic conditions. Upgrading generation facilities, transmission lines, and distribution networks to withstand extreme weather events minimizes the risk of outages. Structural reinforcements, improved design standards, and advanced materials help protect assets against floods, storms, and heatwaves. Relocating critical infrastructure away from high-risk zones such as coastlines or floodplains further reduces exposure. Integrating resilience criteria into planning and permitting processes ensures that new projects are designed to endure future climate conditions rather than historic averages.

Diversification of energy sources enhances resilience by reducing dependency on any single fuel or supply route. Expanding renewable energy portfolios, including solar, wind, hydropower, and geothermal, mitigates exposure to fossil fuel market volatility and geopolitical supply disruptions. Distributed energy systems, such as microgrids and decentralized generation, provide localized reliability during system-wide failures. Integrating diverse energy technologies allows systems to adapt to fluctuations in resource availability and demand, strengthening overall stability.

Energy storage plays a key role in enhancing resilience and supporting adaptation. Storage systems such as batteries, pumped hydro, and thermal storage balance short-term supply and demand fluctuations, ensuring continuous power availability. During disruptions, storage can provide emergency backup for critical services, including hospitals and communication networks. Long-duration storage and the use of hydrogen as an energy carrier offer additional flexibility for managing seasonal or prolonged shortages. Investing in storage capacity strengthens the ability of energy systems to operate under stress and recover quickly after disturbances.

Digital technologies and data analytics improve resilience through predictive monitoring and rapid response capabilities. Smart grids equipped with sensors and automated control systems enable operators to detect faults, isolate affected areas, and restore power efficiently. Advanced forecasting tools that integrate weather data and demand patterns support proactive maintenance and system optimization. Digital twins and simulation models allow planners to assess system vulnerabilities and test adaptation strategies under various scenarios. These technologies enhance operational awareness and decision-making, reducing the likelihood of cascading failures.

Institutional coordination and governance are essential for effective adaptation. Collaboration among energy, environment, and emergency management agencies ensures cohesive responses to disruptions and consistent policy direction. Developing national frameworks for energy resilience integrates risk assessment, contingency planning, and resource allocation across sectors. Regulatory bodies can require utilities to implement resilience plans and conduct regular stress testing of systems. Clear communication protocols between governments, operators, and the public enhance preparedness and improve recovery efficiency after extreme events.

Financial instruments support investment in resilient and adaptive energy systems. Governments and financial institutions can establish dedicated funds, insurance schemes, and incentives to promote infrastructure hardening and risk reduction. Climate finance mechanisms and green bonds can be directed toward adaptation projects that enhance system robustness and reliability. Integrating resilience criteria into investment assessments ensures that funding decisions reflect long-term risks and sustainability objectives.

International cooperation strengthens resilience by facilitating knowledge exchange and regional coordination. Cross-border energy interconnections enable countries to share resources during shortages and emergencies, reducing dependence on single national systems. Joint research initiatives on climate-resilient technologies and materials expand the global capacity for adaptation. Multilateral development banks and international agencies provide financial and technical assistance to support developing countries in building resilient energy infrastructure.

Community-level engagement contributes to local energy resilience by promoting decentralized solutions and awareness. Training programs and capacity building improve the ability of local operators and residents to manage disruptions effectively.

Community-based renewable energy projects enhance self-sufficiency and ensure access to critical services during crises. Public awareness campaigns encourage energy conservation and preparedness measures, helping to mitigate demand spikes and reduce strain on the grid.

Energy resilience and adaptation strategies require continuous evaluation and adjustment as risks evolve. Incorporating resilience into every stage of energy planning—from design and investment to operation and governance—creates systems capable of sustaining reliable performance amid environmental and socioeconomic uncertainty.

Supply Chain Security and Critical Minerals

Supply chain security and the availability of critical minerals have become central concerns in the global energy transition. The shift toward renewable energy technologies, electric mobility, and energy storage systems has created new dependencies on specific materials, including lithium, cobalt, nickel, copper, and rare earth elements. These materials are essential for batteries, wind turbines, solar panels, and electric motors, yet their production is geographically concentrated, exposing global energy systems to supply risks, market volatility, and geopolitical tensions.

Critical mineral supply chains are characterized by high concentration at various stages, from extraction and processing to manufacturing. A few countries dominate the mining of key materials, while refining and processing capabilities are often located elsewhere, creating interdependencies across borders. This uneven distribution increases vulnerability to trade disruptions, political instability, and natural disasters in key producing regions. The reliance on a limited number of suppliers also amplifies market power imbalances, enabling price manipulation and supply restrictions that can disrupt clean energy technology deployment.

The extraction of critical minerals poses environmental and social challenges that influence supply chain stability. Mining operations can lead to habitat destruction, water contamination, and carbon emissions, while in some regions, they are associated with poor labor conditions and community displacement. Growing scrutiny from consumers, investors, and regulators has intensified pressure on producers to adopt responsible sourcing practices. Certification schemes and traceability systems are being developed to ensure transparency and sustainability throughout the supply chain, helping reduce reputational and regulatory risks.

Diversifying sources of supply is a key strategy for improving critical mineral security. New mining projects in underexplored regions, including parts of Africa, South America, and Asia, can reduce dependency on existing producers. However, developing these projects requires long lead times, substantial investment, and stable regulatory frameworks. Expanding domestic production capabilities and processing capacity in consuming countries can also reduce exposure to external shocks. Governments are increasingly prioritizing mineral independence by incentivizing local refining and manufacturing through tax benefits, subsidies, and strategic partnerships.

Recycling and circular economy approaches play an important role in mitigating supply risks. Recovering metals from end-of-life batteries, electronics, and renewable energy components can reduce the need for new mining and lower environmental impacts. Advances in recycling technologies are improving recovery rates for critical materials such as lithium, nickel, and cobalt. Establishing efficient collection systems and industrial-scale recycling facilities requires coordination between manufacturers, policymakers, and waste management sectors. Circular approaches can extend resource lifespans and strengthen material security while supporting decarbonization objectives.

Strategic stockpiling offers an additional safeguard against supply disruptions. By maintaining reserves of critical minerals, governments and industries can buffer short-term shocks resulting from geopolitical conflicts, trade restrictions, or natural disasters. Strategic reserves must be managed carefully to avoid market distortion and ensure availability when most needed. Transparent criteria for stockpile release and replenishment help maintain market stability and investor confidence. Some countries have established public-private partnerships to manage reserves collaboratively, balancing national security with market efficiency.

Technological innovation contributes to reducing material intensity and diversifying inputs. Research into alternative materials and substitutes for rare and high-risk elements can reduce dependence on specific minerals. For example, battery technologies are evolving toward chemistries that use less cobalt or nickel, while permanent magnet development is exploring rare-earth-free designs. Efficiency improvements in manufacturing processes also lower material consumption and waste generation. Investment in research and development supports technological resilience by widening the range of viable material options.

International cooperation is essential for stabilizing critical mineral supply chains. Multilateral frameworks, such as the International Energy Agency's Critical Minerals Initiative and the Minerals Security Partnership, encourage data sharing, standard setting, and joint investment in responsible mining projects. Collaborative efforts to improve transparency, environmental governance, and labor standards can build trust and reduce supply chain vulnerabilities. Supporting capacity building in developing countries that host mineral resources ensures that benefits are more evenly distributed and that local communities share in the economic opportunities created by the energy transition.

Private sector engagement plays a major role in improving supply chain security. Companies are increasingly assessing and managing their exposure to mineral risks through diversification strategies, long-term contracts, and supplier partnerships. Due diligence requirements, sustainability reporting, and environmental, social, and governance (ESG) standards are being integrated into procurement and investment decisions. Collaboration between industry and policymakers can align market incentives with sustainability goals, promoting secure and transparent supply chains for the clean energy technologies of the future.

Geopolitical Dimensions of Energy Security

Energy security is closely linked to geopolitical dynamics, reflecting the influence of geography, politics, and economic interdependence on energy supply and demand. The global energy system operates within a complex network of trade routes, resource distribution, and international relations. Access to energy resources has historically shaped foreign policy decisions, economic alliances, and regional stability. As countries pursue secure and sustainable energy futures, geopolitical factors continue to determine the risks and opportunities associated with energy transitions.

The concentration of fossil fuel reserves in specific regions has long been a source of geopolitical leverage. Major oil and gas exporters have used energy supply as an instrument of influence in international relations. Dependence on imports exposes consuming nations to supply disruptions and price volatility resulting from political conflicts, sanctions, or instability in producing countries. Strategic chokepoints, such as the Strait of Hormuz, the Suez Canal, and the Strait of Malacca, amplify these vulnerabilities, as disruptions to maritime trade can have immediate global repercussions.

Energy interdependence between producers and consumers creates both cooperation and competition. Exporting countries seek stable markets and revenue streams, while importers prioritize reliability and diversification. Long-term contracts, joint ventures, and cross-border pipelines have historically fostered collaboration but also deepened political dependencies. Shifts in energy trade patterns, driven by the rise of new producers and alternative supply routes, are reshaping geopolitical relationships. For example, liquefied natural gas (LNG) trade has introduced greater flexibility to global gas markets, reducing dependence on specific transit routes and suppliers.

The energy transition introduces new dimensions to geopolitical competition. As countries invest in renewable energy, electric mobility, and digital technologies, demand for critical minerals and manufacturing capacity has emerged as a strategic priority. Control over the extraction, processing, and export of key materials, such as lithium, cobalt, and rare earth elements, is now central to global economic influence. Nations with strong positions in clean energy manufacturing, such as solar panel and battery production, are gaining new forms of strategic leverage.

Technological leadership in low-carbon energy systems is becoming a determinant of geopolitical power. Countries that dominate renewable energy technology, hydrogen production, or advanced grid systems can influence global standards and supply chains. Intellectual property, innovation capacity, and investment in research and development provide competitive advantages that shape global markets. The ability to export clean energy technologies and services is emerging as an important component of diplomatic and trade strategies.

Energy transitions also have implications for traditional energy exporters. Economies heavily dependent on oil and gas revenues face the challenge of diversifying income sources while maintaining social and fiscal stability. Declining global demand for fossil fuels may alter geopolitical hierarchies, reducing the influence of hydrocarbon-rich states. At the same time, exporters investing in renewable energy and hydrogen are repositioning themselves as future energy suppliers, adapting to maintain strategic relevance in a decarbonizing world.

Regional energy integration can enhance security and cooperation but also introduce new dependencies. Cross-border electricity interconnections, shared gas pipelines, and regional power pools facilitate efficient resource use and system stability. However, they also require political trust and coordinated governance. Disputes over water resources, shared infrastructure, or unequal access to energy benefits can strain regional relations. Effective governance mechanisms and transparent agreements are necessary to ensure mutual benefits and prevent political conflict.

Climate policy is increasingly influencing geopolitical relations. International commitments to reduce emissions, such as those under the Paris Agreement, are shaping trade, investment, and industrial policies. Carbon border adjustment mechanisms and environmental standards may affect global competitiveness and trade flows. Countries with abundant renewable resources are positioned to export green energy, while others may face challenges in adapting to changing regulatory and market conditions. The intersection of climate diplomacy and energy policy is redefining global alliances and rivalries.

Energy security in a multipolar world depends on managing the intersection of traditional and emerging geopolitical risks. The transition toward cleaner energy sources does not eliminate competition for resources or influence but shifts it toward new domains such as technology, infrastructure, and materials. Building resilience in this evolving landscape requires diversification, cooperation, and adaptive governance that account for the changing geopolitical realities of the global energy system.

Conclusion

Energy security remains a cornerstone of sustainable development and global stability. It underpins economic growth, social progress, and environmental protection, connecting closely with the Sustainable Development Goals. As the world transitions to cleaner energy systems, the definition of energy security continues to evolve, encompassing not only access and affordability but also resilience, inclusivity, and sustainability.

The changing energy landscape presents both opportunities and risks. Rapid advances in renewable technologies, digital systems, and energy efficiency provide the means to reduce dependency on fossil fuels and strengthen resilience against supply disruptions. However, these shifts introduce new challenges related to critical mineral supply chains, infrastructure adaptation, and equitable access to technology and finance. Policymakers and industry leaders must balance short-term energy needs with long-term sustainability objectives through coherent strategies and coordinated governance.

Achieving universal access to reliable and modern energy remains essential for social and economic inclusion. Electrification, clean cooking solutions, and decentralized energy systems contribute to poverty reduction and improved quality of life. Expanding access requires mobilizing investment, supporting innovation, and addressing affordability barriers in low- and middle-income regions. Inclusive energy policies must ensure that the benefits of technological progress reach all communities, especially those most vulnerable to climate and economic shocks.

Energy transitions depend on robust governance and effective international cooperation. Transparent decision-making, regulatory consistency, and cross-sectoral coordination build trust and enable collective progress. National energy strategies aligned with global climate commitments can guide investment toward low-carbon pathways. Strengthening institutions and capacity in developing countries supports equitable participation in global energy markets and fosters resilience to external risks.

Investment in innovation and infrastructure forms the foundation of future energy systems. Emerging technologies such as hydrogen, carbon capture, and digital energy management can accelerate decarbonization while enhancing flexibility and reliability. Integrating resilience into design and planning ensures that infrastructure can withstand physical and systemic shocks. Financing mechanisms, including public–private partnerships and green finance instruments, are critical for scaling these solutions globally.

The geopolitical landscape of energy is undergoing transformation as renewable resources, technology, and data reshape international relations. While new dependencies are emerging, they can be managed through diversification, transparency, and cooperative frameworks. Global efforts to stabilize supply chains, promote responsible sourcing, and harmonize standards will determine the security and sustainability of future energy systems.

Energy security and the SDGs share a common goal: ensuring that development is inclusive, resilient, and environmentally sound. Realizing this vision requires long-term planning, sustained investment, and an integrated approach that connects energy with water, food, climate, and economic systems. Through collaboration and innovation, countries can build secure energy systems that support prosperity while safeguarding the planet for future generations.

www.ingramcontent.com/pod-product-compliance
Lightning Source LLC
Chambersburg PA
CBHW052139270326
41930CB00012B/2949